Deceitful Practices

DECEITFUL PRACTICES

Nomura Securities and the Japanese Invasion of Wall Street

John E. Fitzgibbon, Jr.

A BIRCH LANE PRESS BOOK
Published by Carol Publishing Group

A Birch Lane Press Book
Published by Carol Publishing Group
Birch Lane Press is a registered trademark of Carol Communications, Inc.

Editorial Offices: 600 Madison Avenue, New York, N.Y. 10022
Sales & Distribution Offices: 120 Enterprise Avenue, Secaucus, N.J. 07094
In Canada: Musson Book Company, a division of General Publishing
    Company, Ltd., Don Mills, Ontario M3B 2T6

Queries regarding rights and permissions should be addressed to Carol Publishing Group, 600 Madison Avenue, New York, N.Y. 10022

Carol Publishing Group books are available at special discounts for bulk purchases, for sales promotions, fund raising, or educational purposes. Special editions can be created to specifications. For details contact: Special Sales Department, Carol Publishing Group, 120 Enterprise Avenue, Secaucus, N.J. 07094

Manufactured in the United States of America

10 9 8 7 6 5 4 3 2 1

Library of Congress Cataloging-in-Publication Data

Fitzgibbon, John E.
    Deceitful practices : Nomura Securities and the Japanese invasion
  of Wall Street / by John E. Fitzgibbon, Jr.
      p.   cm.
    "A Birch Lane Press book."
    Includes index.
    ISBN 1-55972-098-0
    1. Nomura Shōken Kabushiki Kaisha—Corrupt practices.
  2. Securities industry—Japan—Corrupt practices. 3. Securities—
  United States. 4. United States. Securities and Exchange
  Commission. I. Title.
  KNX1064.F57   1991
  345.52'0268—dc20   91–27252
  [345.205268]   CIP

To those who mean the most to me
Connie
Lisa and Jennifer

Contents

Introduction

I'VE BEEN AN ITINERANT WALL STREETER ALL MY LIFE, AND proud of it. I was born into a semi-Japanese society in 1932 in Honolulu, the son of a naval officer. As you might expect in such a family, I grew up and traveled all over the world—three continents, fifteen countries, forty-four states. I attended an exhausting twenty-six different schools. My brevity record was set during the one week I spent at Bishop England High School in Charleston, South Carolina. If I learned anything there, I don't know what it was. My favorite, though, was the famous Swiss boarding school LeRosey, where I learned to ski and ice-skate and sat beside the present Aga Khan in Latin class.

The Wall Street life always suited me just fine. Working at such solid, respected firms as Merrill Lynch, Paine Webber, and Smith Barney, I thought I had gotten a sound grounding and a good feel for the arcane ways of the investment world. And, barring the occasional bad apples, I thought I knew the ethics of the Street, how far anyone would stretch to make a sale or eke out a commission. During my peripatetic travels as the son of a navy man, I learned one hard and fast rule for survival: Obey the other guy's rules and expect him to obey yours. But the day came when I found myself staring at something none of my experience had prepared me for.

No brokerage house is mightier than Japan's Nomura Securities, the world's biggest investment firm, many times the size of Merrill Lynch and twice as large as the entire American brokerage industry. *Fortune* magazine once remarked that Nomura could swallow Wall Street like sushi, and indeed it could. Among its many distinctions, it is one of the most profitable companies in the world. When the United States needs to finance its awesome budget deficit, its most benevolent customer is Nomura Securities. Experts are convinced that international finance will soon be controlled by a handful of global banks, and Nomura is the bettor's choice to lead the pack. It was with great trepidation, therefore, that the American brokerage fraternity watched as Nomura opened an American operation in 1953 to compete for Wall Street's dazzling riches. But for a number of reasons, the new outpost didn't really amount to much until around 1970, when it deliberately set about recruiting American professionals. I was the first American—*gaijin* or outsider—hired as an officer by NSI. Its board of directors elected me an assistant vice president two days before I reported for work.

I came to Nomura thinking I would be assisting a diligent, shrewdly managed company in becoming an important competitor to Wall Street's established houses. I believed I would be part of a gust of competition that would sweep away some of Wall Street's inefficiencies. The first few years at the firm, however, I was stunned by Nomura's laughable ineptness. The behavior of the Japanese, totally befuddled by American ways, reminded me of a Marx Brothers movie, and I sniggered along with each scene. I frankly thought Nomura would have a hard time competing with a college investment club. About the only way the operation could have made money then was if it found it on the street.

As the years rolled by, I also discovered that the Japanese at Nomura Securities International didn't at all respect American securities regulations and laws. Time and again, I found them systematically flouting the rules that Wall Street lived by. When stock and bond deals could not be sold, Nomura used its vast network of foreign affiliates by illegally slashing prices through a kickback-of-commissions scam to get the issues sold. As a result, many of our own companies such as Merrill Lynch, Goldman Sachs and others were unable to compete as NSI dumped those stocks and bonds at reduced prices in violation of the American securities laws. On one occasion, it flooded the American markets with issues that were never registered for sale in this country. More important, this crooked dispersal of securities played a role in pushing up American borrowing rates to scandalous levels, including having a severe effect in the capital markets where our home mortgage rates reached 17 percent in the late 1970s. Perhaps Nomura's American affiliate thought this the way to succeed at business, though in the end it didn't prove to be. It kept right on slipping on banana peels.

I was pressured to go along with these dirty doings, but I refused, a decision that pushed me into the lower reaches of the firm and ultimately out the door. And that led me to write this book in the hope that revealing what goes on at Nomura would serve as notice to those who jump into bed with Japanese brokers. Look before you leap!

The Nomura manipulations warrant exposure if for no other reason than their pervasiveness. The present-day scandals that have engulfed Wall Street are one-dimensional—insider trading and parking of securities—and have been connected to a mere sprinkling of professionals. Virtually all of the manipulations, in fact, have stemmed from a single individual: Ivan Boesky. Normura's shady activities are more multifaceted and have been carried out on orders from its senior management. Its wrongdoings go back at least twenty years. To the best of my knowledge, they continue to this day. Some of them may seem technical and arcane to the layperson, but so did insider trading before Ivan Boesky and Michael Milken made the practice infamous.

In large part, this book is about what it is like to be an American in a Japanese company, a truly singular experience that has never really been chronicled. Even in the United States, you find yourself subjected to gross prejudice that becomes intolerable.

But in another sense, it is a story about cultural differences and protection of the American marketplace. Many barriers exist to entry into Japan's lucrative markets. But while we sit still for these exclusionary practices, we go ahead and not only open our doors to the Japanese, but give them advantages by not enforcing the laws that Americans like Ivan Boesky and Michael Milken get put in prison for breaking.

We've all heard so much about how the Japanese are infallible at just about everything they do. If they wished to get the upper hand in the disposable diaper market, most people would bet they would get it. Indeed, much of American business has come to shudder at the mere mention of the Japanese and to endow them with almost magical and mystical powers. This is a story that reveals a rather different side to the Japanese. It is about a Japanese behemoth that couldn't seem to get anything right. In trying to achieve success, it didn't rely on enviable management techniques or shrewd motivational practices. It broke the rules.

I have tried to tell the tale of Nomura's invasion of Wall Street largely in the framework of the years I worked for the company, during the early to late 1970s, and observed them from close range. What Nomura did in those years constitutes an important lesson for today, one that has never been taught. My Nomura experience, in many respects, serves as a magnifying glass to focus all that is wrong with Japanese and American relations. Everything in this book I either personally witnessed or had confirmed to me by actual participants in the events. It is an insider's book by someone who has worked for Japanese brokers for nearly twenty years, by someone who knows how it was—and only wishes it hadn't been.

Acknowledgments

My twenty-five-year friendship and association with Louis Vincent Riggio resulted in this book. Lou likes to claim the dubious distinction of bringing me into Nomura Securities International, and, indeed, he did. Once on board, he helped guide me through NSI's minefields, as far as it was humanly possible. And when the time came to tell the story of Nomura's invasion of Wall Street, Lou rolled up his shirtsleeves and went to work on the task. I can truly say, if a man has just one person to call a friend, he is blessed. I am so blessed.

Also, a special acknowledgment to Al Barbara, Dan Burstein, Fred Coleman, the late Joan Cromwell, the late Dick Gibson, Larry Gurwin, Annabelle Krigstein, David H. Kogut, Dennis and Mary Kronyak, Sue Sawyer, and Paul Zerler. A special thanks to my editors Hillel Black, Jeff Mitchell, Donald J. Davidson, and India Cooper, and Philip G. Spitzer, my agent, who put this project over the top.

Finally, to "The Unknown Soldiers" who wish to remain in the shadows: You know who you are and I am forever grateful to you because none of this would have been possible without your help and support.

Deceitful Practices

Prologue

O_{N JUNE 22, 1988, IN A CAVERNOUS CONFERENCE ROOM} near Kabuto-cho—Tokyo's version of Wall Street, where Japanese hope and despair were regularly realized—a flock of institutional investors gathered for a bond seminar. Among those who showed up were distinguished emissaries from Japan's largest banks and insurance companies, a veritable Who's Who of global financial powers.

The center of attention, and the magnet that drew the investors, was unquestionably the host, the fabled Nomura Securities Company, Ltd., and the meeting was in actuality more a command performance than a traditional seminar. At the close of the session, after hours of hearty backslapping by Nomura, the company had a little suggestion for the invitees. It recommended that they invest in American government bonds. Specifically, the group was urged to buy the U.S. Treasury 9⅛ percent bond, maturing in 2018, which was presently selling at a little over 100 a bond. As it happens, the unbeatable investment value of the bonds had nothing to do with it; the advice was given, in the explanation of the host, because "Nomura alone would push the market price up to 101¾." In other words, the iron will of Nomura could be counted on to create its own value.

The bonds did in fact begin to surge that day in Tokyo, but, disappointingly, they failed to attain Nomura's predicted closing price. Nothing to worry about. There was always the New York marketplace.

Halfway across the globe, six hours later, the curtain rose on the New York market. U.S. government securities started the session languidly, with their prices little changed from the previous day's close. The targeted bond was unchanged at 100⁶/₃₂ (government bonds are traded in units of one-thirtyseconds of $1,000). But as the hours ticked past, the picture

3

changed dramatically. Fourteen hours after Tokyo's close, the U.S. Treasury market soared and Nomura's pick, the 9⅛ Treasury, hit the predicted price of 101¾, thus gaining nearly $17 per $1,000 bond for the day. That was like the Dow Jones average exploding by 100 points. Multiplied by the thousands of bonds being traded by big holders, the increase in the price translated into plentiful profits of hundreds of thousands of dollars.

Nobody at Nomura, of course, was the slightest bit surprised by the fulfillment of the prophecy. They knew full well how mighty they were. Power had spoken, and June 22 went down in Tokyo as "Nomura Day."

1

Another *Gaijin* Joins Nomura

RIGHT FROM THE START, EVEN BEFORE I WENT TO WORK there, the place struck me as odd. It took a while for it to become truly scary. My first encounter came one sun-drenched spring day in early May 1973, when as a forty-one-year-old seasoned Wall Street professional I stepped off the elevator onto the sixteenth floor of 100 Wall Street and, as I would later describe it to friends, wandered straight into the Twilight Zone. That would become my pet name for Nomura Securities International.

I have to admit, the place itself looked ordinary enough, not all that much different from the innumerable brokerage house offices I had been in and out of. Dark green carpeting snuggled the floor of the reception area, and ceiling fixtures kept the room murkily lit. A few spindly plants stood in corners, and some traditional Japanese pictures comprised the sole effort to embellish the walls.

Nomura Securities International, or NSI as it was commonly called, was the American affiliate of the Nomura Securities Company, Ltd., of Tokyo. Though still pretty much unknown in this country, Nomura was nothing less than the mightiest securities firm in Japan, the rough equivalent of Merrill Lynch here if you could imagine the place that's unshakably bullish on America being six or seven times larger. And through the New York–based NSI it was bent on becoming as formidable a factor in America as it was in Japan. Indeed, its grand ambition

5

was to dominate all of world finance. Who could say it wouldn't? By 1973 everybody was getting the unmistakable message that whatever the Japanese wanted to do, they did.

I was greeted by NSI's receptionist, Agnes Minejima, a short and stocky, unfailingly pleasant older woman who spoke both Japanese and English fluently and had been with Nomura longer than anyone could remember. Before the year was out, she would be hustled into retirement, because the president thought the company's receptionist ought to be young, fetching, and American, not somebody's Japanese grandmother.

I was shepherded into the office of Yoshio Terasawa, then president of the small American affiliate who in 1981 would become its chairman. His incessant glad-handing had already made him known as Japan's Ambassador of Goodwill to Wall Street. He bore a smile that spread from ear to ear, and he always introduced himself by saying, "Call me Terry."

Terry was in his early forties, a graduate of Waseda University, a polished gentleman, and a cultural contrast to the typical Nomura man. He spoke good English. He stood about five-foot-six, kept his jet black hair combed straight back, and was a little roly-poly.

Once I was seated, an old friend named Lou Riggio, a thirty-five-year-old wry and erudite Wall Streeter who had been hired by NSI about three years earlier, joined us. At the time I was working elsewhere on Wall Street, but I had been counseling Lou on a matter he was puzzling over that could be rather important to Nomura's future. The day was coming when foreign membership would be allowed by the New York Stock Exchange, and Terry wanted Nomura to be in a position to be the first to join. There were two obvious options. One was to wait and jump into the footrace with all the other Japanese firms, but this left too much to chance. The other was to buy into an existing member.

The latter option gave birth to my Riggio & Company proposal, which I was here to present to Terry. My suggestion was that Nomura set up an American company for the purpose of buying a seat on the NYSE and staff it with a few trusted people like Lou. NSI would then feed this company enough business to keep it alive and breathing. The day the exchange's rules changed, NSI would simply acquire Riggio & Company.

Presto, Nomura would be the first foreign member of the New York Stock Exchange.

Terry liked the idea and gave it his stamp of approval. All that had to be done was to iron out the details. For reasons unknown to me, Nomura never put the proposal into action. That day, however, fully believing they were going to push ahead with the plan, Riggio suggested that I join NSI. With me on board, everybody could work together and the Japanese staff at NSI could get to know me better. Terry liked that idea as well and asked me if I would be interested. I told him I would.

At that point, Terry motioned for Riggio to step out of the room during the salary discussions. The money agreed on wasn't all that much, but it was in line with what NYSE member firms were paying their branch office managers.

Before everything was finalized, Terry wanted me to meet with Masaaki Kurokawa, the company's senior corporate finance vice president, and Harunobu Aono, the corporate syndicate vice president. Typical of the Japanese, Terry needed a consensus to hire me, and Kurokawa and Aono would constitute it. An appointment was arranged for the following afternoon.

When I arrived, I was waved into the chairman's office. While I sat on a sofa, the two Japanese flopped into armchairs on either side of me. Kuro, as he liked to be known, was a six-footer, though like many people of above-average height, he slouched. I would later learn more about Kuro. Like most Japanese, his marriage had been arranged and he kept what scant family life he had very private. Kuro had graduated from Kyoto University and then spent a year at the University of Wisconsin, where he learned to speak English and swig beer. He used to brag that he never attended classes and that he purchased a car and brought his wife over from Japan in defiance of Nomura's corporate policies. Kuro came from rural Japan, a fact that his fellow workers never let him forget. He had a dark complexion, black hair, and dark eyes. Even his name was dark-hued; in Japanese, *kurokawa* means "black river." He was a terrific salesman who knew his product. But he was also a bully with a vulcanized tongue and a powerful sadistic streak. The Americans who worked at NSI liked to say that he made Rambo look like Tinker Bell. Kuro was crafty enough to know where to draw the line with superiors. With subordinates, Japanese or American, it didn't matter. He was an equal opportunity abuser.

Aono, on the other hand, was a peppy, good-natured man whose main function at NSI was to serve as a shield between Kuro and the rest of the staff. In his spare time, he headed the corporate syndicate department. Aono was a butterball and, at just over five feet tall, a good foot shorter than Kuro. The two of them, however, were inseparable and were commonly known as "Mutt and Jeff."

Kuro cleared his throat and thanked me for coming. He looked terribly uncomfortable, as if he were a little sick to his stomach. After a few more innocuous remarks, he remembered something he had to do and sprinted out of the room.

I was left with Aono, who was fidgeting like a man too embarrassed to scratch an itch. He and I sat staring at each other, faces blank, struggling to think of something to say to break the deafening silence. After a short while, Kuro mercifully returned. Unfortunately, he couldn't think of anything more to say, either. Aono abruptly remembered something of vital importance and departed.

The staring bout continued now between Kuro and me. Shortly Aono reappeared, and then Kuro said he was needed outside for a moment. Aono winced and apologized for the confusion by saying, "It can't be helped." That's the expression the Japanese often use when things go wrong, a fatalistic acceptance of misfortune.

The door opened, Kuro entered, and he thanked me for coming. I was ushered out to the elevator, and when it arrived and I was tucked safely in, Mutt and Jeff gave me a respectful deep bow.

I had spent less than eight minutes with the two top Japanese officers and had barely heard them utter a word. I must confess, I was a little taken aback. Maybe this was why nobody in this country really knew who or what Nomura was. What was I getting into?

Riggio, in fact, had told me earlier about an embarrassing contretemps that should have been a good clue to what life was like at NSI. One day the Tokyo parent asked NSI to recommend "the stock of all stocks" to buy for its domestic clients. Riggio was handed the task. He was very taken with Merrill Lynch, since, among other things, it was selling near the year's low of $15, down more than 50 percent from its high of $32. Thus the stock had all the requisites for the Japanese investor: a low price, a respected name, an undervalued position in the marketplace. Because there was no written research available from Wall Street on stock brokerage firms, Riggio had to visit Merrill and write one up for Nomura.

After the report was circulated, orders flowed into NSI from Japan to buy Merrill Lynch shares. The orders got heavy enough to push volume in the stock to about ninety thousand shares a day, double its normal level. The buying spree also began to shove up the price. Within a few months, it neared $20 and Tokyo began taking profits. In short order, Nomura became the major seller of Merrill Lynch.

Somehow a young *Wall Street Journal* reporter heard that there might be something cooking within Nomura having to do with Merrill Lynch. He made a call to try to learn what it was. As it turned out, the reported dialed the wrong telephone number and got a man named Naomichi Shimao in the sales department, one of the nameless, faceless junior people from Tokyo.

Shimao knew that Japan was buying some Merrill Lynch stock, but that was about all he knew. His job was to sell Japanese stocks to American investors. Nevertheless, he tried to be as helpful as possible to the reporter. When he didn't understand a question, he simply said, "Yes." What the reporter didn't know was that his reply was the classic Japanese "yes." Whenever a Japanese fails to comprehend a remark, he or she says "yes" as an acknowledgment, meaning nothing more than that he or she heard the question and didn't know the answer. Well, the yeses fairly quickly added up to what the young reporter concluded was the scoop of his career. Before long, the story came clattering over the Dow Jones wire that Nomura was in fact going to buy Merrill Lynch.

All hell broke loose, and the Securities and Exchange Commission even launched an inquiry, soon aborted, into the incident. Nutty stuff like this, Riggio told me, always seemed to be happening at NSI. Riggio called the SEC investigator with answers, but waited until 4:45 P.M. Friday. Lou said the man never called back.

By this point in my life, though, I thought I was overdue for a new adventure. I had had a fairly peripatetic career in the securities business. In the fall of 1956 I began my Wall Street life when I joined Merrill Lynch's office in the far-off place of Zanesville, Ohio (famous for having the only Y-shaped bridge in the country; to get to town, you came rumbling east on U.S. 40 and made a right turn in the middle of the bridge). At the time, the Dow Jones average looked a mite high as it approached 600. Around the office, spittoons were in popular demand. When I called potential clients and identified my firm, most of them thought we were lawyers.

In February 1963 I switched to the Park Avenue office of the stock brokerage firm of Harris Upham & Company as a registered representative and later moved up to manager's assistant. Several years later, Lou Riggio joined the same office. Our director of research was a memorable character named Ralph Rotnam, who in one year correctly predicted both the Dow Jones high and low to the precise dollar. He earned his place in history, however, as the author of the Hemline Theory, which argued that the stock market rose and fell in tandem with skirt lengths. The higher the hemline, the higher the stock market, and vice versa.

Despite the whimsy, the Harris Upham research approach was decidedly conservative. It was rare that any client would get hurt, but opportunities to catch a shooting star were equally rare. So unless a salesperson had hundreds of clients, this philosophy didn't make for meaty monthly commissions. Most brokers, including Lou Riggio, didn't enjoy such a broad base and had to cast about on their own for creative ways to make a buck.

Riggio's late grandfather, Vincent Riggio, had once been the highest-paid executive in America as chairman of the American Tobacco Company. Riggio earned a degree from Yale and two graduate degrees from Columbia. He served in the U.S. Foreign Service and worked in the visa division in the Caribbean before returning to the States in early 1964. He was nearly six feet tall with dark hair and hazel eyes. Though his grandfather left a sizable estate, it was well divided among the family or tied up in trusts. Riggio was pretty much on his own to make something of himself.

Shortly after Riggio came to Harris Upham, he attended an alumni dinner held by the Columbia Graduate School of Business. Next to him sat an old acquaintance from his student days, Kanju Sugimoto. Riggio remembered him as the guy who rarely spoke yet earned the highest grades in the class. Sugimoto worked for Nomura Securities.

In the mid-1960s the Tokyo stock market had slipped into what could best be described as a four-year period of consolidation. A combination of events had brought this about. President John Kennedy had imposed a tax on the purchase by Americans of foreign securities, the interest equalization tax. It effectively knocked U.S. investors and their millions of investment dollars out of all foreign securities markets for the next twelve years. The real coup de grace for the Tokyo market was the collapse of Japan's largest brokerage house, Yamaichi Securities. The Japanese government and the Bank of Japan had to rescue it from bankruptcy, and it ceased to be the dominant factor and sank to number four in the rankings. Nomura, which had been second, backed into first place. The interest equalization tax essentially idled Japanese brokers in this country, and just about all of them reduced their offices to two or three people—except Nomura. It felt that this action by the American government wouldn't last, and it wanted to be ready to dominate the future flow of investment dollars into Japan.

After the two old acquaintances met at that dinner, Sugimoto began sending Riggio information about the Tokyo stock market, and Riggio was quick to perceive that it was grossly undervalued and the cheapest buy of any securities market. Listening to Sugimoto, he in time started adding such names as Canon, Toyota, Hitachi, and Fuji Photo to his recommended list of securities, despite the tax. Slowly, Riggio's clients began to nibble at these strange-sounding names. Any who stuck with them for the long haul made fortunes.

In mid-1968 the Europeans suddenly woke up to what Riggio already had discovered and stormed into the Tokyo market with their buying shoes on. They came with such explosive force that the result was one of the wildest buying binges ever

seen. The funny-sounding stocks went into orbit. Some dou-
bled and tripled within a matter of weeks. Riggio's fame swiftly
spread among his clients and spilled over to their friends.
Harris Upham was besieged by a mass of people opening new
accounts to buy Japanese stocks.

As it turned out, this marked the beginning of the end for
Riggio at Harris Upham. About this same time, the U.S. stock
market had gotten caught up in a speculative binge of its own,
led by low-priced, low-quality stocks, and was about to top
out. Harris took measures to cool off such dealings by imposing
a house rule that no commissions would be paid to any salesman for buying a stock selling for less than $5 a share. Since the
preponderance of the Japanese stocks sold in that price range,
Riggio was just about put out of business. Then certain people
in Harris's main office learned of Riggio's growing volume in
Oriental stocks. They didn't much like it, and he was ordered
to cease such activities. Left to depend upon Harris's sleepy
research department, Riggio's business declined so drastically
that the manager of the office felt compelled to do something.
He asked Lou out for lunch. This event was known around the
office as "the long walk to Bruce Ho's."

Bruce Ho's has been on East 57th Street between Park and
Lexington for years. Whenever a salesperson was invited to
lunch there, it meant only one thing: the end. Often the victim
would be put on notice, meaning he or she had a few months
to produce incredible volume or find a new job. Under the
circumstances, few of those invited had any stomach left for
lunch, so the tabs were pretty small.

Riggio was infuriated. Knowing the potential for Japanese
securities, he phoned Sugimoto and arranged for a meeting
with him and Yoshio Terasawa. The company's capital base
had just been raised to $3 million from $1.5 million, and NSI
was ready to make its move. Two branch offices were already
in place, one in Los Angeles and the other in Honolulu. They
were staffed by Japanese nationals and several locals, usually
female Japanese or Japanese-Americans. It took a lengthy number of meetings before Riggio was finally offered a job, but on
January 12, 1970, he became the first American professional
hired by the New York operation.

About six months after Riggio left Harris Upham, I too took a new job, as the assistant manager of the international division of the brokerage house of Eastman Dillon Union Securities. One of my functions was to service the investment needs of the local foreign affiliates, including the Japanese houses. Through Riggio's introduction, I got to know Nomura and they became familiar with me. Eastman Dillon was run as a partnership from the Roaring Twenties, with each partner guarding his turf, though in time the firm gave way to the professional managers of Paine Webber. I left there after a while and wound up at the carriage house firm of Dominick & Dominick, where I worked as the assistant manager of the New York office. The firm was heading into rough waters that would result in massive cutbacks and layoffs. I would be gone before that happened. From the first day that I started with Dominick, the Japanese staff of NSI and Lou Riggio regularly called me for counsel. Because Dominick's international department covered the account, I got no commissions from my work. It didn't matter. I got something that I thought was worth a lot more: a new job.

When I reported for duty at NSI, I was assigned to a cramped alcove where a few filing cabinets had to be shoved aside to make room for me. When I thought about it, my work space wasn't all that bad. Riggio made do with a walk-in closet. Once I settled in, I decided to get straight to work. The only problem was, what work? After whiling away some time drumming my fingers on my desk, I caught Riggio's attention and hissed, "Pst! Lou, what am I supposed to do?"

He glanced up from his paperwork and replied, "Sit back and relax. This place is more like the civil service than Wall Street. Work will find you, you don't have to look for it."

The working conditions were indeed vastly different from any I had previously encountered. I had spent more than twelve years in retail branch offices, where the telephones were always ringing, the salespeople were scampering back and forth to the order window, the customers were jockeying for the front-row spectator seats to watch the ticker tape, and the office boy (usually a tottering old fogey) was trooping past the salespeople's desks dropping off the never-ending research reports. Now I was sitting in an isolation booth waiting for the $64,000 question: What to do?

Riggio, however, was right. Work did eventually find me. One by one, the Japanese began to gravitate to my desk for consultations. At first it was hard for me to understand what they were talking about, because their English was so bad. But how could I complain? My Japanese didn't exist. I couldn't even say, "Nice day out." Had I been the foreigner working in Japan, I wouldn't have been able to locate the men's room.

The initial questions the Japanese had for me were pretty elementary stuff. What did this statement in the *New York Times* mean? Did I know this stockbroker? How did I interpret this research report? Once the Tokyo staff got to know me a little better and knew I wasn't going to tattle about how laughably ignorant they were of American ways, the flow of questions turned into a veritable flood that kept me busy well after the local *gaijins* stampeded past me and out the door at 5:01. Who knew? Maybe life at NSI was going to be interesting after all.

2

Nomura Grows Up

From the very beginning Nomura seemed to know it was destined to make unusual things happen. The company's roots go back to 1872, just four years after the Meiji Restoration, when a far-sighted man named Tokushichi Nomura, the illegitimate son of a samurai, opened a money exchange house in Osaka. At the time, Japan was shifting to a modern industrial society, and innumerable businesses were being spawned by former samurai. As this new company grew, it appropriately became known as the Osaka Nomura Bank.

Steady but relatively uneventful expansion transformed it into a fairly substantial regional institution. The company received its first major break when the imperial government canceled all of its war contracts at the end of World War I. This dealt a crushing blow to industrial and financial activities throughout Japan, and all the Japanese trading companies, or *zaibatsus*, suffered brutal reverses. Luckily for Nomura, it had positioned itself more prudently than the others. It remained safe, sound, and solvent, and to become even more solvent, it exploited the opportunities that beckoned and assumed a dominating presence in its home territory of west-central Japan, known as the Kansai Region. The bank wrung a vast amount of business from many of its competitors, including the famous Sumitomo Zaibatsu. These two groups remain spiteful and belligerent rivals more than seventy years later.

By 1918 Nomura had been reorganized into a holding company called the Nomura Gomei Kaisha, and it was poised for still further improvement in its fortunes. During the Roaring Twenties the Japanese securities market mimicked the upward direction of Wall Street. Stocks and bonds became seductive investments, and a surge of business caused a heady ascent in prices. It was a period of dramatic expansion that put wide smiles on the faces of Nomura employees. During its early days, the Osaka Nomura Bank's securities operations were primarily centered in bonds, and by 1925 this area had grown so large that it was spun off from the bank to become the Nomura Securities Company, Ltd. Present-day Nomura people thus tend to think of 1925, rather than 1872, as the year their company came into being.

While it grew fat and sassy in its home country, Nomura began eyeing new frontiers. The propaganda of the other top Japanese securities firms notwithstanding, Nomura has always been the pacesetter in the overseas markets. The company opened its first foreign office in 1927 in New York City's Equitable Building, well ahead of the competition. This milestone was celebrated in a company song: "The Japanese flag is hoisted in the morning breeze on Wall Street / And the Statue of Liberty smiles upon / Our truly global power."

During its formative years, the New York office never actually sold any securities but functioned chiefly as a listening post to glean information about Wall Street that could be used by the Tokyo parent in its trading in Japan. Even in those days, the American markets affected securities activity in Tokyo.

But Nomura's global power didn't last long. The business activities died out in the early thirties, and the office was closed at the outbreak of World War II. And with the Japanese surrender in 1945, the country's domestic securities markets came to an abrupt halt.

To the amazement of the Occupation Forces, Japanese securities circles proposed that trading resume by the end of the year, a mere four months after the signing of the capitulation. The Occupation, though, couldn't be bothered. It had its hands full restructuring the Japanese economy and public life. This work included the destruction of the *zaibatsu*, and Nomura Gomei Kaisha was one of the designated targets. Therefore, the importunings of the brokerage industry to reestablish itself were ignored until 1949, when over-the-counter trading was allowed to resume on a limited basis.

Among other things, the dissolution of the *zaibatsu* eliminated the Nomura family from top management roles and split Nomura Gomei Kaisha into pieces. The Occupation ordered that either the bank or the brokerage company, but not both, could retain the Nomura name. The securities firm won the coin toss, and thus the Osaka Nomura Bank became known as the Daiwa Bank, not to be confused with the Daiwa Securities Company, Japan's second-largest stockbroker. (In English *daiwa* means "great peace.") The securities company emerged as the bearer of the old company pennant, and most former family members gravitated to it to a greater or lesser extent.

There's a curious footnote to all this. Despite the efforts of the Allies to stamp out the *zaibatsu*, "Nomura Gomei Kaisha" continued to be a legally registered business in Brazil. Who knows? Perhaps the Occupation's measures didn't translate well into Portuguese or reach as far as South America.

The firebombing of Japan by the American Army Air Corps during the war virtually leveled the country. All traces of the former economic system were in ruins. Japan's industry had to rise from that rubble and try to rebuild itself from scratch. The country was devoid of capital and, desperately needing foreign exchange, funneled its energy into manufacturing finished goods for export. It made enormous demands on its citizens, and they unstintingly responded. The Japanese worked hard, made countless sacrifices, and methodically squirreled away their wages under their mattresses.

Obviously, Japan needed bucketfuls of money to fund its economic recovery plans. To pitch in and do its part, the Nomura sales force was flushed out of its offices and dispersed into the countryside. It operated with a diligence that bordered on obsession. In fact, a Nomura salesman's success wasn't measured by the volume of his commission business but by how long it took him to mutilate a pair of shoes. The salesmen rapped on the door of every Japanese household they could get to, trying to cajole housewives to sink their savings into Japan's future.

It was a perfectly plausible strategy. In the Japanese home, the husband dutifully handed over his pay envelope to his wife and entrusted her with managing the house and the family. She in turn gave him an allowance to cover his personal expenses and maybe a little mad money too. Although Japan has always been an extraordinarily male-dominated society, the women have traditionally kept a tight fist on the family's purse strings.

To capitalize on this feature of home life, Nomura set up a "part-time" sales force to assist its full-time employees and serve as its front-line contact with its customers. This contingent was composed of middle-aged housewives, known as "midis." They were not your normal part-timers. They worked a backbreaking eight-hour day, yet they didn't get any of the company perks or the promotions that the Nomura men did.

Effective they were. Starting in 1953, the midis swarmed throughout Japan carrying piggy-bank-like savings chests into the local neighborhoods. The Japanese housewives were encouraged to save by plunking every spare coin into the chests, and then, when the piggy banks were full, the midis would return to collect the money. Eventually, more than one million such chests found their way into Japanese homes. Of course, the midis kept the only key to the savings chests to make sure no one had any second thoughts about her savings should she happen to spy some really gorgeous kimono in a store. Once the midis handed over the stashes to Nomura, the money inevitably found its way into the stock market. This sales campaign continued until 1962, when it was replaced with equally successful Tupperware-like parties. There was little doubt about it: Nomura, through its earthy door-to-door sales approaches, knew how to bring the Japanese capital markets to the public.

Measured in sheer money terms, Nomura Securities was unquestionably the major beneficiary of the demise of the *zaibatsu*. Its principal brokerage competitors were smaller pieces of the other *zaibatsu* and remained very much under the spell of their past. Thus, although the Japanese brokerage industry was generally referred to as the Big Four—Nomura, Daiwa Securities, Nikko Securities, and Yamaichi Securities— Nomura was to a large extent a Big One. The four firms dominated the trading on the Tokyo Stock Exchange and accounted for about 50 percent of the daily volume, yet Nomura's share by itself became slightly more than 20 percent. Nomura, moreover, was the only pure broker. Daiwa was a satellite of Sumitomo Bank. Nikko was a satellite of Mitsubishi Bank. Yamaichi was linked to Fuji Bank. Thus Nomura represented itself and had no restrictions on its movements. It answered to no one.

As Japanese industry grew, Nomura grew merrily along with it. Its expansion, however, was entirely in its own marketplace. Even today the company collects nearly 90 percent of its revenues, and almost all of its profits, from the Japanese markets. Although the foreign affiliates have become quite large in their own right, the international side has never been a significant contributor to the parent's overall net income.

The main reason is the singular attitude of the Japanese. Any Economics 101 class teaches its students the theory of "guns and butter." You can have one or the other, but not both. If you make guns, you will have a buildup of cash, but nothing to spend it on. Too much currency will chase too few goods. This inevitably results in inflation. The Japanese, however, turned this theory on its head. Because Japan's postwar economic policies were oriented toward export rather than personal consumption, the country's capital base kept swelling right along with the personal savings of its citizens. The population was encouraged to save, save, save—and given tax breaks and other incentives to make sure it did just that.

By offering the Japanese myriad ways to invest their savings, Nomura Securities quickly became one of the major factors in the redeployment of Japan's capital. Like other financial institutions, it built a huge flow of capital and took a nick out of each transaction for itself. By any measure, it knew the home market and controlled it. Overseas, where people's attitude toward money was radically different, Nomura was on shakier ground.

After an absence of nearly two decades, the Nomura Securities Company, Ltd., reopened its New York City representative office in 1953 at 61 Broadway. During the next few years, two more representative offices were opened in the United States, one in Los Angeles and another in Honolulu. For the next sixteen years, it busied itself becoming reacquainted with the marketplace, gleaning intelligence, selling a few Japanese securities, and occasionally doing some underwriting. In 1969 Tokyo upgraded these offices to become affiliated companies, and they were incorporated in the State of New York as Nomura Securities International, Inc. The Nomura Securities Company, Ltd., owned 95 percent of NSI's common stock and the Bank of Tokyo the remaining 5 percent. By the early 1980s, the Bank of Tokyo had sold its holdings back to the Nomura Securities Company.

NSI began life in the United States with some twenty-five employees, a capital base of $1.5 million, and two branch offices. (Twenty-one years later, that capital base had expanded to $375 million, the number of employees had risen to 547, and NSI had four branch offices, in Chicago, Los Angeles, San Francisco, and Honolulu, though the latter two were closed in 1991.) Its major ambition at first was to sell Japanese securities to American investors and participate in Japanese stock and bond underwritings. At this juncture, it had only a fleeting interest in other areas. Moreover, it didn't really care whether it made five dollars or five million. What mattered was to build a presence. Profits could come later.

The people Nomura sent to staff its American outpost were not necessarily the finest talent it had groomed. Because most of Nomura's business was with the Japanese public, the road to its senior management came from the ranks of domestic retail salesmen, not from Nomura's international investment bankers. Inside the company there were cliques. Because the Japanese are group-oriented, allegiance is to the family and to the company, and not necessarily in that order. Within the company an employee aligns himself or herself with a smaller group, and then these minigroups joust among one another. Those who were shuttled overseas often seemed to be the ones who didn't fit in. To be sure, some talented people were sent abroad, but for some reason they just didn't belong in the mainstream of Nomura Securities.

No matter where a Nomura man served, though, his report card was graded in Japanese. A's were hard to come by. The company has always been unforgiving, and even the slightest mistake, one failed spot quiz, could and did ruin a career. Success belonged to the group; failure was an individual matter. What's more, Nomura was always looking for ways to ambush people on the narrowing road to the firm's directorship. Thus, when a Nomura man was sent to a foreign country, he continued to be thoroughly Japanese. In the long run, this approach in the United States was to serve neither the individual nor the company well.

The year 1970 was certainly the turning point for the Japanese brokers. It marked the beginning of their move into power and dominance in the arena of international finance. Some of history's most far-reaching developments began with a minor happening that went virtually unnoticed at the time. On April 15, 1970, the Japanese Ministry of Finance allowed Japanese mutual funds to invest $40 million in foreign securities, and thus Japan started to export its capital. The initial commitment was not all that huge, but what stood behind it, if all went well, were untapped billions.

The context in which Japan began to pour money into this country was important to succeeding events. The speculative fever that swept through the American stock market during the late 1960s had come to an end, and stock prices were in full retreat. The stocks that led the way down were the cheap issues that had been in the forefront of the upward charge. The blue chips got bloodied, but not nearly as much. Thus when the Ministry of Finance originally gave the go-ahead for Japanese mutual funds to internationalize their investment portfolios, it was the blue chips on the New York Stock Exchange to which they were restricted.

The market's slide came to an end by the middle of 1970. The Dow Jones average stood at 710 in July, and prices started to creep back up until six months later they surpassed the 900 level. So the Japanese had caught the U.S. market perfectly. Had they moved into Wall Street a year or two earlier, they would have been sitting on the top of a bull market. Inevitable losses would have followed, and perhaps the Japanese would have retreated to Tokyo to lick their wounds for another decade. But 1970 was the ideal time to make an expansion move. Luck was in the air.

Nothing breeds success like success, and because of the joyful results of the first wave of money that washed into the American stock market, the Ministry of Finance further liberalized overseas investments. Indeed, from this first splash, a tidal wave of billions of dollars would flood the international securities markets. And the Big Four of Japanese brokers had the inside track to the money. Nearly 80 percent of the original amount was earmarked for the New York capital markets. Wall Street made plans for a banquet, and the Japanese were the unmistakable guests of honor.

Since the only stocks that the Japanese could purchase in the United States had to be traded on the New York Stock Exchange, and since foreign membership was not permitted on the NYSE at that time, the Americans were fighting to get in line to grab some Japanese stock business. They came bearing all manner of gifts. They showered the Japanese brokers with securities research and gave them free access to their superstar securities analysts, a privilege accorded to only a few and never to a competitor. The Japanese were afforded sharp commission discounts that only giant institutions could demand. Japanese visitors were given guided tours of the American brokerage offices. They were entertained royally, and underwriting invitations flowed like rainwater. In short, the Americans gave the Japanese brokers every possible opportunity to make money in the U.S. markets. The Japanese were spoon-fed from the day the order flow began in Tokyo. Quite naturally, American firms hoped for an equal opportunity to do business in Japan.

The Japanese brokers took full advantage of these munificent gifts. They played the Americans off against one another. Many on Wall Street today feel the Japanese never came close to returning the favors. By 1987 only three U.S. brokers had been permitted to buy a membership on the Tokyo Stock Exchange. The following year another six were granted membership. Only a handful of American investment firms have been allowed into Japanese underwritings, and those instances constituted token gestures more than anything else.

The American securities markets are built on reciprocity: I'll scratch your back, you scratch mine. The Americans compete vigorously with each other, but they also pitch in and help each other out. All the Merrill Lynches and Salomon Brotherses wanted from the Japanese was an equal opportunity to compete in one of the largest and richest securities markets in the world. But they never got it. The Americans gave away the store and got nothing for their generosity. The Japanese were handed positions as primary dealers of American government securities over the objections of the Congressional Banking Committee. Did it open the Tokyo securities markets? No. In 1990, after eight years of fruitless negotiations with the Japanese to pry open the Tokyo markets, the U.S. Treasury charged the Japanese with discrimination.

The way the Japanese were courted for their orders in the early 1970s could make anybody's head swell. But these orders were not where the game was as far as the Japanese were concerned. Make no mistake about it, the chief reason they had come to the United States was to promote and sell their own product: Japanese stocks and bonds. Sales, after all, gave the Japanese the rare opportunity to execute business on the Tokyo Stock Exchange on behalf of Americans. Thus any American broker with some Tokyo stock business to hand out was besieged by the Japanese.

By and large, however, the American public was only interested in U.S. stocks, and at times there wasn't even enough of that business to feed all of Wall Street. There always seemed to be a few anorexic firms. So in early 1970 none of the major Japanese brokers boasted a staff of more than twenty-five people in the United States. Their sales volume simply didn't require any more bodies.

Despite the apathy they faced, most of the Japanese stationed here worked very hard to drum up sales, sometimes to ludicrous extents. I'll never forget one encounter I heard about. The head trader of a NYSE member firm's trading desk called a Japanese broker to get the price of a stock traded on the Tokyo exchange for one of his branch offices. The man obligingly found the price, and the trader relayed it to the branch. About an hour later, the receptionist called the trader to say he had visitors. When he dashed out to the waiting area, there stood three Japanese businessmen. One was the supervisor from the firm he had just called. He was accompanied by his research analyst and his trader. They had arrived armed with volumes of reports on the stock in question, as well as on many other Japanese securities. After some deep bowing, they left the bewildered American trader with the huge stack of papers.

Even though the early years were lean and endlessly frustrating for the Japanese affiliates, they never relinquished hope.

They hung in there. Unlike most American brokers, the Japanese had a long-term game plan, and they kept to it religiously. It would take time, but they had time. It would take capital, but they had capital. It would take work, but they had an enormous capacity for work.

Lou Riggio had demonstrated a knack for selling Japanese stocks to American investors, which is what had brought him to the attention of Nomura. When he joined NSI in 1970 as its first American broker, the little business the company did came from a small band of brokers. What NSI wanted from Riggio, as well as any other Americans it hired, was for him to dig up customers so the Japanese salesmen could then service them.

A few days before Riggio started his new job, the Tokyo Stock Exchange took a spill, followed by a precipitous plunge. The decline was touched off by guidelines issued by Federal Reserve chairman Arthur Burns limiting how much American institutional investors could invest in foreign securities markets. The money that was already invested overseas could stay put, but new dollars leaving the country were severely restricted. Because U.S. institutions were the fastest-growing segment for sales, the Japanese companies had pinned their hopes on nurturing this business. Now it was gone.

Despite this gloomy development, and for who knows what reason, NSI felt it ought to go blithely ahead with its game plan for rounding up new business. Hence Riggio was dispatched with a team from Tokyo on a whirlwind tour across the country to promote the very investment that Chairman Burns had all but banned. Riggio zigzagged his way from New York to Boston to Los Angeles to San Francisco.

Even though Riggio returned home empty-handed, NSI considered his excursion a smashing success. As far as his superiors were concerned, it was enough that he had arrived back with a humongous expense account and the names of a few new people he had visited. After all, he had waved the Nomura flag around the country, and that's what counted. NSI at this juncture was judging results by mileage, not dollars.

By the time I joined up in the summer of 1973, NSI had about three hundred of what it considered to be customers, not counting those on the West Coast, who were serviced by the

Los Angeles office. (Except for Honolulu and the West Coast, everything in this country was handled by the New York office.) In actuality, just thirty of these three hundred clients had opened accounts and done some business with NSI. All anyone else had done to qualify as a customer was to have been approached by a NSI salesman. From the time Nomura reopened its American operations in 1953, it was averaging a bit more than one new account per year. I guess this period of time can best be summed up as a lot of wing-flapping and very little flying.

Riggio's next assignment was to be the contact man with Wall Street in order to set up the machinery for the flow of Japanese money to be invested in American stocks. This task brought him into contact with all the greats and near greats of the American investment community. This was a logical job for him. After all, there were only a few Japanese at NSI, and they were busy promoting unwanted, restricted securities to nonexistent customers. Besides, Riggio was the only one who could speak English well, who understood American sales techniques, and who knew the way American brokers operated. So Riggio spent his next few months making the rounds and opening the accounts to handle the business.

Then something strange happened. Assistant Vice President Hiroshi Kawanaka, a barrel-chested man who cut his hair in a flat-top that made him look more like a marine sergeant than the assistant operations manager of NSI, asked Riggio to lunch. They went to a grungy Chinese place not far away from the office. It was judged a discreet setting, since it was not the sort of place that many competitors were likely to patronize. In fact, the only people who ate there had cast-iron stomachs and a cavalier attitude toward life.

The luncheon proved to be a difficult East-meets-West encounter. Riggio didn't speak Japanese, and Kawanaka was just learning English. Kawanaka started out by asking Riggio if his marriage had been arranged. Lou felt he dropped a few notches in the Japanese man's estimation when he admitted it had not been. Yet the two hit it off, and as Kawanaka's English improved, so did his friendship with Riggio.

Some months after that first lunch, Kawanaka approached Riggio with a problem. It seemed that there was some difficulty with a transaction in a convertible bond of Komatsu, Ltd., the earthmoving equipment maker, that had been issued previously in Europe. Securities laws require any security traded in the United States to be registered with the Securities and Exchange Commission. As with all rules, there are exceptions. One exception is "seasoned securities," stocks or bonds that have been traded in the international markets longer than 270 days. The Komatsu bonds weren't registered and didn't fall under the seasoned securities guidelines. Thus they weren't authorized for sale in the United States or to U.S. citizens. Soliciting business in unregistered securities is a major violation of American securities laws.

According to Riggio, Kawanaka told him that NSI had sold these bonds to an American institution and now needed documentation to prove that the trade fell under the registration guidelines. The signature of a registered principal on the papers was required, and so Riggio was asked to sign them. Had the transaction been proper, the document would have already been filled out, lacking only a signature. What was put down in front of Riggio was a completely blank form. The tumblers clicked in Riggio's head; he knew something was definitely out of order. He refused to pick up his pen.

Instead, he told Kawanaka to fill in the required information and then bring the form back for his signature. Kawanaka returned with the form still blank. At last, he explained that it couldn't be completed because it represented an improper transaction. Riggio winced, but he stood his ground and refused to sign the paper. After that, there was little meaningful dialogue between Riggio and Kawanaka. At this point, Riggio didn't know if this was just some isolated foul-up or if it was symptomatic of how the Nomura people went about their business. He wasn't entirely sure he wanted to know the answer.

Riggio, however, kept getting pretty choice assignments. Nomura's interest was by no means limited to the United States, for the parent was quietly developing a worldwide corporation whose tentacles reached into Latin America. Since Spanish, Portuguese, and English are the principal languages spoken south of the American border, and since Lou spoke, wrote, and read all three of them, he was given coverage of the Americas.

In that capacity, Riggio did much of the spadework upon which Nomura's foundation in South America would be built. He made inroads in every significant country—Brazil, Mexico, Venezuela. Nomura was so far ahead of all the other major Japanese banking firms that he encountered little competition. It was a dream way to operate.

Because Riggio's work in Latin America was starting to become profitable, Masaaki Kurokawa, NSI's senior vice president and head of corporate finance, saw fit to become interested in the area too. Kuro took a trip with Riggio to visit these countries, hoping to promote his own Nomura career.

Kuro noticed right away that the South Americans were having a tough time pronouncing "Kurokawa." It has never been a good idea for a businessperson, especially one staking out a new territory, to have a tongue-twister of a name; you want something that rolls easily off the customers' lips. Kuro decided he would Latinize his name to put his clients at ease. He insisted on being called "Culo." Kurokawa simply changed the *K* to a *C*, and in Japanese an *R* often sounds like an *L* anyway. When Riggio heard this, he had to stifle his laughter. *Culo* is the Spanish word for "asshole."

Naturally, the nickname spread like wildfire among the *gaijin* staff at NSI; they could never bear to miss an opportunity to call Kurokawa "Culo-san." He always answered.

Back in those days, you could never tell what NSI was going to get mixed up in. During the spring of 1972, Riggio returned from one of his missionary trips to South America, and Yoshio Terasawa, the president, summoned him to his office. Terry was practically bursting with excitement. It seemed he had an offer he couldn't refuse, a humdinger of a deal. NSI had been approached by a group of businessmen wishing to finance the development of a horse track in Pennsylvania. The name of the property was immediately familiar to Riggio; he had read about it in the newspapers in connection with a Cosa Nostra scam. Unwittingly, NSI was all set to go into business with the Mafia or get taken to the cleaners.

When Terry finished breathlessly telling Riggio about the proposal, he asked him whether he thought it was a good idea, fully expecting to hear a resounding yes.

"No," Riggio said at once, and explained why.

Terry frowned. He had a problem. The introduction had come through the daughter of NSI's chairman. How could he tell the boss that his daughter had goofed? Worse still, how was he going to tell the old man that he had goofed too?

Terry tried to argue that maybe the deal was legitimate, but Riggio convinced him that if he liked remaining among the living, he had better turn down the offer. Winding up at the bottom of some harbor didn't appeal to Terry, so he finally capitulated, though Riggio was the one who wound up having to confront the businessmen with the bad news.

3

The Cotton Affair

ALTHOUGH I WAS OFFICIALLY SUPPOSED TO REPORT FOR work on May 21, 1973, I was asked to begin a couple of days earlier. This allowed me to be drawn into an ill-fated mess that became known around NSI as the Cotton Affair. It also gave me an early and telling reading on the judgment of my new employer.

DB Cotton & Associates was an investment counseling firm situated on Florida's Gold Coast. Donald B. Cotton had founded the company three years before to cater to the not inconsequential investment needs of the wealthy who lived and played (mostly played) in the area. The going had sometimes been painfully slow for the firm, but it apparently had managed to eke out a certain amount of success.

Don Cotton had brought an interesting background to Florida. Some years earlier, he had written a book about his theories of business management that happened to catch the attention of one of the senior officers at Coca-Cola. As a result, Cotton was hired to breathe some more life into the soft drink company. By Cotton's telling, his approach had been a mite too radical for the rest of the arch-conservative Coke management team. A minor palace revolt by the senior executives resulted in the termination of Cotton's contract much earlier than he had expected. He got a handsome settlement, however, and took the money and moved to Florida.

Somewhere along the line, Cotton had managed to strike up a friendship with the then-chairman of Nomura Securities in Japan, Minoru Segawa. At the time, Segawa was the most

29

influential individual in the Japanese financial community. He was equal in stature to Jim Robinson, the chairman of American Express, Bill Schreyer, the head of Merrill Lynch, and John Gutfreund, the chairman of Salomon Brothers, all rolled up into one. It was hard to fathom what the two had in common. Cotton kept to himself and liked to stay in the background, ready to step forward when needed, traits he undoubtedly picked up from being an admiral's aide. Segawa, on the other hand, was a bulldog of a man with a face to match. Socially, he was kind, gentle, and sincere. Underneath that soft velvet glove, however, was a fist of steel that could strike a fatal blow without warning. Believe me, he was tough. He had to have been to rise to chairman of the board of Nomura. Softies wouldn't get halfway there.

Despite these differences, Segawa and Cotton had a mutual respect for each other and a solid friendship. Among other things, Segawa had taken a distinct liking to sunny Florida and its tabletop-flat golf courses. They were ideal for keeping your score down, and Segawa liked low scores even more than most golfers. Consequently, Cotton made arrangements for Nomura to purchase a house for Segawa's use in Fort Lauderdale.

The price of the house had been $175,000, a pretty preposterous sum in 1973 for anything short of a plantation. The real estate agent had insisted it was an absolutely fair price, though I presume her definition of fair was whatever generated the highest commission for her. She dispelled all my doubts when she insisted she could have a firm bid on the table to buy the house from Nomura for $250,000! And by the following day. It made me think twice about the stock brokerage business.

Because of Cotton's chummy relationship with Segawa, any time Cotton had a proposal for NSI, it was to be taken with the utmost seriousness. If he wanted to sponsor frog races with Nomura, you took a good look into the popularity of frog races. My first assignment at NSI was to explore Cotton's latest brilliant idea, which was that NSI buy DB Cotton.

I was instructed to make an appointment that Saturday afternoon in Fort Lauderdale with DB Cotton & Associates. Lou Riggio would accompany me on my adventure. Terasawa told me to inspect the company thoroughly and return to New York with one of three decisions. The first choice was to accept

Cotton's offer for NSI to buy the company. The second was to recommend giving Cotton a bit of money to manage; something on the order of $250,000 was the figure in mind. The third choice was to reject the other two proposals. Knowing of Cotton's relationship with Segawa, this hardly struck me as a simple assignment. On the other hand, I didn't imagine it would be all that difficult. Unless Cotton's firm was teetering on the verge of imminent collapse, I assumed the only sane recommendation was the first choice.

Just in case I needed any assistance in coming to that conclusion, I was offered a blunt hint before I left. Terasawa pointed out to me that Merrill Lynch had just acquired the investment firm of Lionel D. Edie, and now NSI had a chance to do pretty much the same thing. "This could be just like Merrill Lynch and Lionel Edie," Terry said.

I couldn't be sure whether Terry was trying to make it easy for me to recommend the acquisition for political reasons or if he actually was convinced the deal had some true merit. Being Japanese, he gave no clues. What a way to start a new job!

I caught a Saturday morning Eastern Airlines flight to Fort Lauderdale. I had on a business suit, and when I glanced around me, I realized that everyone else was wearing a double-knit leisure suit except for a couple of women. Riggio had gone ahead so he could spend Friday night with his parents in Palm Beach, and he met me at the airport. We checked into the Pier 66 Hotel and Marina, which boasted a revolving dining room on the sixteenth floor, a chancy place if you happen to be a heavy drinker. We went up to my room, and the phone soon rang. It was Don Cotton. He was waiting in the lobby.

No matter how many times you looked at Don Cotton, and no matter from how many angles, it was hard to tell how old he was. A blond man with a fair complexion and a luxurious Florida suntan can easily conceal the accumulation of years. My initial guess was that he was somewhere between his late thirties and early forties, but I realized I could be off by anywhere from five to ten years. A beanpole, he stood six-foot-two and weighed 140. In 1973 he was still quite the eligible bachelor.

Cotton was decked out in a blue blazer, light gray slacks, loafers, white button-down shirt, and a dark tie. He sure looked like he belonged on the Gold Coast. He showed us to his car, which belonged there too. It was a brown four-door Mercedes in mint condition.

The offices of DB Cotton & Associates occupied a suite in the International Building, a modern Florida mid-rise structure set near the ocean in Fort Lauderdale's high-rent district. The decor unquestionably lived up to the rent. Awaiting us was the company's vice president of administration and treasurer, Neil Burmeister. Don Cotton showed us his plush office at the end of the hall and gave us a speedy tour of the premises before shepherding us into a large conference room where the meeting would be held.

After delivering a general briefing on the company, Cotton laid out his proposal: NSI would buy DB Cotton & Associates for $300,000; as part of the deal, NSI would have to guarantee the investment firm an annual budget of $200,000 for at least three years. What's more, the Nomura family was to steer investment money from its worldwide sources to the Cotton company to manage. All told, Cotton was asking NSI to commit $900,000 to an operation it would then have to support.

That might have been a perfectly acceptable sum, or at least somewhere in the ballpark, if DB Cotton & Associates had been rolling along in rosy shape. In actuality, it was clinging to a life raft by one fingernail. After three years of operation, all it had to show for itself were fourteen accounts. Cotton was reluctant to tell us the exact amount of money he had under management, except to complain that clients were habitually slow in paying their fees. He said he wanted to drop all of them except one, who happened to be a good friend whose money Cotton managed for free. About the only selling point of the company was that it had a license as an investment advisor in Florida. It was true, of course, that NSI would get to acquire Cotton's assets—which amounted to the office furniture and all of $5,000 in the bank, maybe enough money to cover two months of operations. So what Terasawa had conceived of as a glorious million-dollar opportunity was looking to be more like a two-cent opportunity.

There was one more small consideration. Cotton made clear that in his own contract with NSI it was to be stipulated that he would report only to Terasawa. That was important to him because Nomura's Japanese staff members normally had a three-to-four-year tour of duty in the States before returning to Japan. Terry was due to be recalled in the near future, and Cotton didn't want to have to deal with some unknown replacement. Thus, no matter where Terry was reassigned, Cotton would still answer only to him. I have to say this much, Cotton was no dope. He had a far better understanding of how to bargain with the Japanese than either Riggio or I did.

But Cotton wasn't quite finished. He said that due to his unique background and qualifications—he was an ex-naval officer, management expert, possessor of extensive knowledge of both Japan and the United States—he was the sole person who could head off the coming war in the Pacific.

What war?

He apparently had this crazy idea that Japan and the United States were headed for another conflict, even though Japan didn't have any arms, and he thought Nomura would be pleased to be associated with someone who could put a stop to it.

The meeting wound up, and Cotton said his good-byes. We would see him but once more. We were put in the custody of Neil Burmeister. A seasoned veteran of Florida financial circles, Burmeister had a winning personality, although his late-model American car didn't quite match Cotton's. He gave us a leisurely guided tour of Fort Lauderdale and then took us to see the famous Nomura-Segawa house.

The single-story, white stucco structure sat back from the street and featured a semicircular driveway. The requisite palm trees dotted the property. The house was U-shaped and huge. The expansive sunken living room had beige wall-to-wall carpet and sliding glass doors leading to a patio and swimming pool. It was sparely furnished: an off-white sofa, huge matching arm chairs, and a glass-topped coffee table. Sitting on the table were two half-empty highball glasses and an ashtray whose contents spilled over onto the table. One glass bore obvious lipstick marks, as did several of the cigarette butts. I could still smell stale smoke in the air. Since Segawa and his wife hadn't been near the state of Florida in at least six months, it was obvious that somebody else was enjoying the palatial splendor of the house.

The remainder of the place consisted of a dining room done up in French provincial, a den, a kitchen, three bedrooms, two bathrooms, and a guest room. The bathroom off the master bedroom had a concession to the chairman. It boasted the usual American fixtures, plus a Japanese-style toilet. I noticed that the king-sized bed in the chairman's room had rumpled sheets that afternoon. Somebody else was making himself at home.

Burmeister took Riggio and me to an Italian restaurant for dinner. We got there around seven and immediately began working on the first round of drinks. We went from beers to Bloody Marys to scotches to several bottles of wine. I had to admit, Burmeister was no slouch when it came to drinking. He was a true pro. In the course of the boozy evening, it emerged that DB Cotton & Associates was on its last legs. In fact, this proposal was Cotton's last-ditch chance for survival.

The Eastern flight back to New York the next day was deadly silent. Frankly, Riggio and I didn't know what to say. We dreaded making our report to Terry. Riggio was wishing he did something else for a living, and I was wondering if it really was too late to get into Florida real estate.

That Monday, my first official day on the job with NSI, Riggio and I made a verbal report to Terry. We didn't pull any punches, but told him the way it was. Given what we had seen and heard, we estimated that Cotton couldn't survive another three months. Hearing this, Terry blanched, and then appeared a touch embarrassed. When Riggio revealed that Cotton's final reason for wanting the acquisition was to head off the coming war in the Pacific, Terry looked like he had just stepped on a nail with his bare foot.

The decision, therefore, was to spurn the offer to acquire Don Cotton's firm. However, Terry couldn't quite muster the courage to deliver the bad news to Cotton. Instead, Riggio had to write a letter to Cotton, then take it into Terry's office and convince him to sign it. Reluctantly, he did.

Don Cotton, however, didn't give up easily. After getting the letter, he put in a hasty call to Terry—collect, naturally—and convinced Terry to see him in New York. Cotton was quite cordial to Riggio and me when he arrived, even though he surely knew we were the ones who had given the thumbs-down on the deal. All in all, he was a nice guy who was desperately trying to salvage his business. After Cotton huddled with Terry for about an hour, to no avail, we joined Terry to walk Cotton to the elevator, the customary treatment for honored visitors. Afterward, Terry told us that Cotton admitted that his business was in a pretty perilous state. Sure enough, the operation folded several weeks later.

And so I got my first taste of the strange ways of Nomura. The incredible thing to me was how so utterly preposterous an idea as the Cotton Affair had gotten as far as it did at what was supposed to be one of the world's leading financial investment firms. Little did I know that in succeeding years NSI was to plunge into messes that made Don Cotton's proposal look like a kindergarten stunt.

4

Vinegar Andy and Me

I WAS ASSIGNED TO NSI'S NEWLY FORMED INSTITUTIONAL sales department. It was not particularly crowded with human beings. It consisted of a staff of just three professionals: Hiroshi Kawanaka, recently transferred from the operations department, Naomichi Shimao, and myself. Our boss was Atsushi Saitoh. (Saitoh was to serve two tours of duty at NSI, the first in the early 1970s and the second in the mid-1980s. By 1991 he had become one of Nomura's ranking officers. Today he is executive managing director of Nomura Securities Company, Ltd., in Tokyo.) During a late summer dinner, Yoshio Terasawa had urged the Japanese employees to coin Western first names for themselves to better get into the spirit of being in the United States. What's more, he felt it would make it easier for them to sell to Americans if a client could call them Felix or Ernie rather than Hiroshi or Atsushi. My department got into the swing of things right away. Shimao began calling himself "George." Atsushi Saitoh selected "Andy." Hiroshi Kawanaka, however, was the one spoilsport. He was not especially enamored of Americans and refused to conform.

Life in the department, I found out soon enough, was not going to be totally smooth, for Saitoh could be a notably contentious boss to work for. Like all Nomura men transferred abroad, he had been tutored in English by an American college professor hired by the company. While in language school, no student was permitted to speak Japanese. If he did, an extra day was automatically tacked on to his instructional period. Andy set the record for penalty days, racking up more than a hundred of them. No one else ever mounted a serious challenge to the mark. He was also famous for changing secretaries at a blistering pace. When he came to the conclusion that he needed a fresh one, usually for reasons difficult to fathom, he would turn viciously on his present secretary and scream at her until she would scamper to the ladies' room in tears. One of the other secretaries would creep back to her desk to collect her belongings.

Once, Andy attended a Nomura-hosted seminar attended by American institutional investors. In a bar after the meeting, Andy sat down beside a beefy American securities analyst and made some crude remarks about a nonexistent fling he insinuated the analyst was having with a new NSI research analyst. The guy hauled back and hit Andy with a roundhouse punch that sent him sailing off his stool and onto his back a good ten feet away. As the rest of us at NSI got to know his bitter personality a little better, we concluded that "Andy" was not a name that did justice to this man. Thus he became known as "Vinegar Andy" out of his hearing.

Vinegar Andy called the first meeting of the new institutional sales force in late August. The session was conducted in the only available space on the cramped sixteenth floor of 100 Wall Street, the supply room. Before the meeting began, the space had to be checked out to make sure none of the clerical people were sleeping there, as was the noontime custom. It was considered bad form to force one of the department heads to step over crumpled bodies on the way to giving a speech.

For some reason, Andy seemed a little nervous. I later gathered that he had no firm idea of what his department was all about. He started off by saying, "The NSI institutional sales department will be successful. We will cover every account in the United States. We will call on accounts from New England to Texas, from New York to Chicago to Philadelphia to anywhere." The talk had plodded on for about five minutes when an embarrassing snore came from behind me. Saitoh's opening pep talk had put Kawanaka to sleep.

Vinegar Andy paused for a moment, ignored the background noise, and then blithely went on.

Later on, when I told Riggio about the meeting, he asked me if the talk had been in English or Japanese. I said it was in

English. Then forget it, Riggio said, the meeting wasn't important and it didn't matter if you were even alive during it. It was
merely a show for the new *gaijin.*

I have to admit I was nervous my first days in the department. After all, the cardinal rule of sales is to know your
product. Well, I knew nothing about Japan other than what I
had picked up from reading the newspapers during World War
II. I knew zilch about its economy, its stock market, or any of
the weird-sounding stocks traded on the Tokyo Stock Exchange. I did know Sony, but as a TV set and a radio.

As it turned out, my ignorance didn't much matter. My
colleagues in the department knew their product very well. But
they didn't know the lay of the land. And that's why they
needed me. At the time, American institutional investors had
no knowledge of or interest in Japanese stocks, so Vinegar
Andy's crew members were more like the pioneers of the Wild
West, slowly inching their way across a strange, uncharted
territory that hopefully led to a better land. Of course, it could
also lead straight into a tribe of angry Indians. My role, therefore, was Indian scout. I was to ride ahead to point the way.
Since this was my land, I was supposed to know how to deal
with the hostile forces.

The way things were set up in the department was somewhat odd by American standards. At American brokerage
firms, the institutional clients (the banks, insurance companies,
and other professional investors) are handled by the sales department according to geographic region. A particular salesman will cover, say, all institutions in New England, another
one will call on banks in the Midwest, someone else will tackle
the South, and so on. At NSI, however, institutional coverage
was divvied up according to the seniority of the salesmen.
Therefore it was not unusual to have more than one person
calling on accounts in the same distant city, even if there were
no more than two or three clients there. You could have, say,
three Japanese salesmen descending on Muskegon, Michigan,
to talk to three banks. A firm rule was that the department chief
always got the most productive accounts; accordingly, he
couldn't help but be the largest producer. Then the next senior

salesman in the pecking order would get the next most productive accounts. This division went on until the most junior man had no accounts at all. That's what I started with when I joined the department—nothing.

Before I could get going on my rounds and try to build nothing into something, however, I received a temporary reprieve from Vinegar Andy. He told me he wanted me to devote my time to finding the "right" person, the decision-maker who doled out the stock business, who should be contacted at each of the myriad institutions we dealt with. Fine. To get started, I asked him for the client list. It was a good two weeks before it crossed my desk. It would hardly have mattered if it had never arrived. It was NSI's mailing list of slightly more than three hundred names. When I glanced at the list, I realized that there was no order to it at all. It was nothing but a mismatched collection of unrelated names. Then I made a startling discovery: The list had been arranged in chronological order and never updated. Compilation of the mailing list had begun years earlier, and the first name that appeared on it was the first person who was ever contacted by Nomura. Some three hundred names later was someone who had been added just a week or so ago. No effort had ever been made to find out whether titles had changed or if people even still worked where the list said they did. In short, nobody had any idea if anything was going to the appropriate people.

Clearly, I had to find a secretary to help me break down and reconstruct the list. This was before the computer became the cherished workhorse of Wall Street, so everything had to be done by hand and typed. Since my assignment was not considered a high-priority task by Vinegar Andy, I didn't get the assistance I really needed. I took me weeks to complete everything, but once I had gotten things in order, I was ready to make my telephone calls.

Getting to use the telephone was a formidable task in itself. NSI had a terribly antiquated phone system, and each department had only a few lines at its disposal. The institutional sales chief and the two other Japanese salesmen dominated the phones in order to make their morning slew of calls. By the time I could slip in and grab a free line, it was noontime, and everybody I wanted to call was out to lunch until two o'clock. When they got back, the salesmen were hugging the phones again.

Once I did manage to squeeze in some productive phone time and get through to people, I began to realize why the Japanese staff wasn't accomplishing much. A case in point was the Girard Bank in Philadelphia. I called the vice chairman there. His name was Bob Williams, and he had graduated from Babson College a year after I did and had been a fraternity brother of mine. I knew I could count on him for a little enlightenment.

According to my list, four Girard people were receiving reports from NSI. From my conversation with Bob, I found out that the first name on the list had retired and the next person had left the bank nearly two years previously. The other two were still with Girard. One was the right person to get the Japanese research, but he was being mailed the calendar of new U.S. underwritings of stocks and bonds. The bank's trading department, not he, should have been getting this material. The fellow in that department was the beneficiary of our Japanese research, which he probably passed along to the nearest trash basket or used to light his cigars. In other words, nobody at Girard was getting NSI mailings that would do them, or NSI, any good.

As I worked my way down the client list, this pattern showed up again and again. I began to wonder how NSI got any business at all.

In time, I finished the job and filed a detailed report with Vinegar Andy. I told him how I had updated the mailing list with current names and ordered things so that for the first time our material would be reaching the right people. As far as I know, he never even looked at it.

A further inkling of how NSI conducted its business came a few weeks later when Vinegar Andy invited me along with him on a trip to Boston. He had a client to call on, and I had my own mission impossible.

My target was Keystone Custodian Funds, a big Boston-based mutual fund management company. Seven months before, Nomura had bought $20 million of Keystone's S-4 Fund, a low-priced mutual fund sponsored by Keystone, for resale in Japan. Not only was this a mammoth order, but it came during a wave of massive redemptions of mutual funds in the United States. Net redemptions in the mutual fund industry are not unlike a run on a bank and can force the closing of a fund. Since this was the first real wave of net redemptions since the days of the Depression, Keystone owed Nomura more than some heartfelt thanks for coming forward with its deep pockets.

In the securities industry at that time, reciprocal business arrangements flourished between mutual funds and stock-brokers. The registered representative, or salesperson, got a commission for selling a mutual fund, and the brokerage house got orders for stocks and bonds for the mutual fund's portfolio. In essence, it was a form of reciprocity. "You sell my fund and I'll give you some stock business. You sell a ton of my fund and I'll give you a ton of stock business." The amount of the reciprocal business varied, but it generally equaled anywhere from one-half percent to 6 percent of the quantity sold by a brokerage house. Therefore, in NSI's case, the $20 million sale of Keystone's fund should have resulted in $100,000 to $1.2 million in commission business from Keystone. Now, in May 1973, the Securities and Exchange Commission had abolished this reciprocal business arrangement, but the Keystone deal had taken place before this prohibition, so the Nomura people were expecting to get their reciprocity. Yet weeks and months kept passing, and the check was still in the mail.

Something had to be done. The Japanese staff did make an effort to twist Keystone's arm, but nothing resulted. So I asked for a shot at Keystone, and NSI readily agreed.

The climate seemed perfect for me to make my pitch. Two weeks earlier, Masaaki Kurokawa, the NSI office manager and senior vice president, had delivered a biting message from Tokyo to his staff that was taken very seriously. (As time passed, nobody paid any attention to such messages.) He underscored the fact that the parent had increased NSI's capital base to $6 million from $3 million, and it wanted results from NSI. Big results. Tokyo expected the subsidiary to start standing on its own feet and not perpetually look to its parent for support. NSI was to produce profits for Tokyo, or things would get very nasty for the people at NSI.

With that message hanging ominously in the air, the Japanese were willing to try just about anything, even giving me my head to try to collect a long-overdue IOU.

Before we got to Keystone, we had to take care of Vinegar Andy's business. He had set up a morning meeting with one of his "customers" in Boston. In these days at NSI, anybody who would speak to you was considered a client. They didn't even have to speak politely. American brokers considered such people nothing more than prospects; customers were people who had actually bought something and were likely to buy more things. But if it weren't for these "customers," NSI wouldn't have had any customers at all.

I referred to these accounts as "nonperforming customers." In banking circles, a nonperforming loan is a debt that is in default of interest payments and principal. Instead of simply writing it off as a loss, which is really what it is, the banks call it nonperforming. That's their own little game of make-believe. With these accounts, NSI wasn't getting any more for its time and effort than the banks got out of those loans. I guess it could have been worse, though. At least we hadn't loaned them money. None, that is, that I knew of.

They didn't come any more nonperforming than David Warren, vice president of the investment advisory company of John P. Chase, Inc., Vinegar Andy's solitary call in Boston. If the name rings no bells, John P. Chase is no longer in business, having been swallowed up by the Continental Investment Company of Decatur, Georgia. Vinegar Andy had been calling on Chase for some time and was still sniffing around for his first order. He was about to discover why the scent never got very strong.

When Andy and I arrived for our ten o'clock meeting, we were shown into David Warren's private office. The windows faced out on the massive glass Hancock Building. That's the one whose glass panes developed the nasty habit of popping out. As we talked, I couldn't keep my eyes off the plywood patches scattered over the façade like postage stamps.

Once we had stuffed ourselves into chairs, Andy sprang into action and gave Warren a rundown on the Japanese economy and several stocks Nomura was touting at the time. I was impressed that Warren was madly scrawling down notes like a court reporter. Yet when Andy strongly recommended that Chase purchase a particular stock, Warren's pen stopped dead and he got evasive. That was when I interrupted and asked Warren where Chase did its Japanese stock business. He said in Zurich, Switzerland, where Chase had its European office. The broker it used was one of our main rivals, Nikko Securities, then the only Japanese broker with an office in that city. Warren said Chase didn't buy foreign stocks in the United States. The interest equalization tax was in place, and Chase's Boston officer would have had to pay a surcharge. That was just great. Warren was getting stock picks from us and then executing the orders through our competitor in Zurich, which got the commissions.

I asked a delicate question: "How can we get paid for our stock recommendations?"

Warren sat there with a blank look on his face and said he didn't know. Apparently, it had never occurred to him that we ought to be paid. Maybe he thought Nomura was some sort of charity, like the Red Cross.

I asked whether Chase had any interest in new issues of American stocks and bonds. Warren brightened and took Vinegar Andy and me into the next office to introduce us to his head trader, a man named Timothy T. Callahan, Jr.

I told Callahan that NSI was becoming active in American underwritings. Perhaps we could do some business with Chase in this area. Callahan wondered what was on our calendar of issues. I mentioned a few possibilities, and one of them caught Callahan's interest. It was a convertible bond, and he gave us an order for a hundred bonds. It was a start, at least. A quick call was placed to NSI's syndicate department and the order was confirmed. Just like that, NSI had an order and a method to do business. The selling commission was $6 a bond, so NSI had picked up $600, which more than paid for our trip to Boston.

We left Chase and headed over to Keystone Custodian Funds. When we got there, we were ushered into the office of Robert Smith, the fund's executive vice president. He was exceptionally polite and understanding, and he should have been. During the meeting, which lasted through lunch, many topics were discussed, but the major subject was the reciprocal business for Nomura's purchase of Keystone's mutual fund. I mentioned that Nomura had managed to sell $20 million of the fund in Japan in a matter of a few days at the same time that Americans were cashing in their funds as if they could spread leprosy. And Keystone had yet to cough up its first dollar of business.

Smith took the unwavering position that Keystone was no longer allowed to offer any business because of the SEC ruling. In a friendly voice, I pointed out that the sales transpired seven months before the SEC action. Then I said bluntly, "It took the parent seven days, or about the same time God needed to create the earth, to place the shares in the hands of Japanese investors. It would take even less time to switch the money into another mutual fund whose management would be somewhat more understanding."

The message was not lost on Smith. But then, just as the dishes were being cleared so we could have coffee, Vinegar Andy put his foot halfway down his throat. For reasons known only (or not) to him, Andy blurted out to Smith all about Tokyo's decree to NSI that it had better start turning some profits and stop relying on Tokyo for support.

Smith smiled ever so slightly. The big bluff had been found out.

The meeting wound up back at Smith's office. All told, we spent three hours with him, and although he had been cordial, the only thing we got for our efforts was a promise that Nomura would receive all of Keystone's Japanese stock business. I got a good sense of what that might amount to when I asked Smith if Keystone was currently doing any trading in Japanese stocks.

"No," he replied.

"Are there any Japanese stocks on Keystone's list of approved securities?"

Again, the answer was "No."

"Well, are there any plans in the immediate future to invest in Japan?" I asked.

"No."

When we left, Vinegar Andy said he considered the mission a tremendous success.

One day in the fall, I learned some more about Nomura's way of doing, or rather not doing, business from a potential client. Kansas City Securities, the broker-dealer arm of Waddell & Reed, a large mutual fund management company, accepted NSI's luncheon invitation to the Broad Street Club, one of Wall Street's snazzy private dining clubs. Sherman Jones, the firm's president, and E. Trice Laird, its head trader, represented Kansas City. Kurokawa was the host, and Vinegar Andy Saitoh and I were invited.

Toward the end of the lunch, Jones told us that our sales efforts were all wrong. There was a specified procedure for doing business with Waddell & Reed, just as there was with all American institutional investors. No stock was going to be purchased that hadn't first been approved by the company's investment committee. In fact, a portfolio manager would be fired for acting on his or her own and buying a nonapproved stock. And the reason there were no orders was that no Japanese firm had made any effort to get a stock onto Waddell & Reed's list. This was the key to open the door, not passing out business cards, stock tips, and free lunches.

To crack the list, Jones said, a broker had to make an appointment with the head of the investment committee to do a presentation. Then the committee would decide whether to add the stock to the approved list. If the stock made the list, the Waddell analyst would follow it and keep portfolio managers advised. It would become the job of the outside broker to keep the analyst posted. Any actual trading in a stock would be up to the judgment of the portfolio managers.

Unfortunately, this sound advice had no takers. Neither Kurokawa nor Saitoh understood what they were being told.

I guess there was just too much of a gulf. In Japan, most stock exchange business was done with individual investors. This type of business was the cornerstone of Nomura's dealings, and the ranks of Nomura's senior management were flush with successful retail salesmen. The Tokyo investor was more apt to buy and sell stocks on tips and stories than on fundamentals (a company's sales and earnings and any new developments pertinent to its business). The American institutional investor, on the other hand, wanted to study a company's annual report before committing pension fund money to a new investment. The Tokyo stockbroker has been known to aggressively pursue an investor to make a sale, up to the point of harassment. But American institutional investors could not be browbeaten with a bevy of telephone calls, so there was no temptation to "churn" their portfolios. If anything, this irksome business approach would result in a broker being dropped by an institution. This was something Kurokawa and Saitoh, both former Japanese retail salesmen, didn't, couldn't, or refused to understand.

Vinegar Andy had supposedly been Nomura's top salesman before coming to the United States. He had risen to the top by calling on individual investors and bombarding them with great stock recommendations. They, in turn, bombarded him with orders. Everybody was deliriously happy. But what worked in the past in Japan wasn't exactly working here. From what I could see, NSI seemed stubbornly determined not to adapt to American ways of doing business. Instead, it would do whatever it took to move securities, without regard to any rules or regulations. As far as NSI was concerned, if it could do it in Japan, it would do it here, and let the SEC be damned.

5

Driving Without a License

During these early times at NSI, a few departments had the potential to make some money, if not the actual ability. One was sales, but unfortunately all it did was relentlessly push droves of unwanted Japanese stocks on consistently uninterested American investors.

The corporate syndicate department was just starting to underwrite American stocks and bonds, but it rarely got any merchandise to sell. When it did get handed some, it had to face the inconvenient reality that it didn't have any customers to sell the stuff to. Hence, it usually lost money. The underwriting profits merely offset some of the inventory losses and kept them from being horribly embarrassing.

The corporate finance department was a solid money-maker, but not in the United States. Because of Lou Riggio's efforts in opening up Latin America, that part of the world was blossoming into a gold mine for NSI.

In fact, the only department that was making any money at all in this country, occasional nasty screwups notwithstanding, was the trading desk—but not in Japanese stocks, in American stocks. The desk operated out of an unglamorous order room, where it routinely carried out the buy and sell orders for Tokyo. It was nice that it was earning profits, all right, but NSI wasn't intended to be the execution arm for the parent's U.S. stock orders. Nevertheless, who was to complain? The desk was a money-making machine for NSI, and in the early 1970s it paid the rent and everybody's salaries. Someone had to. But since that sort of operation didn't make for interesting barroom brag-

47

ging, nobody talked about it, and those who worked in it wallowed in the deepest obscurity.

The traders could be imaginative, I learned. As I previously mentioned, the Japanese Ministry of Finance had ruled that all buying and selling of American stocks had to be executed on the New York Stock Exchange. But NSI discovered another way to collect commissions on its Tokyo-originated American equity business.

Discounting of commissions on the New York Stock Exchange was still in the future—it wouldn't come about until May 1, 1975—but since 1970 the New York Stock Exchange had permitted its members to extend a reduced commission on any order worth more than $300,000. Since most of the orders NSI received from the parent were not nearly that large, NSI wasn't in a position to earn a discount.

There was a way, however, that NSI could itself collect commissions on its Tokyo business. NSI belonged to the Boston Stock Exchange, and under the exchange's rules, the commission business that went to the New York Stock Exchange could be split with another Boston Stock Exchange member. This allowed NSI to recover up to 50 percent of the commissions it handed out to Wall Street.

There had to be better ways to make money, though, so I began to seriously analyze NSI's situation. By 1973 NSI had memberships on three American securities exchanges. It joined the Boston Stock Exchange in 1969, the Pacific Stock Exchange in 1971, and the Midwest Stock Exchange in 1973. Nevertheless, the only exchange it was using was Boston to recapture its Tokyo-originated commissions. The other stock exchange memberships were sitting there idle like trophies on a shelf. If it were possible for an exchange seat to collect dust, these would be buried three feet deep. It occurred to me one day: What is a seat on the stock exchange worth if you are not going to use it?

(As a matter of fact, at one point in the late 1970s, the price of a membership on the Pacific exchange plunged as low as twenty-five cents. That's right, you could buy a seat for the price of a local telephone call. There was a catch, however; the assessments members had to pay would have turned a rich uncle's face ashen.)

There was a brokerage firm on Wall Street that could have been of considerable assistance to NSI in its efforts to make more money, Weeden & Co. It wasn't a New York Stock Exchange member, though it did belong to various regional exchanges. However, it was forging quite a name for itself in what is called the third market. It acted as a dealer for NYSE-listed stocks and executed these orders itself, charging no commission. The establishment (in other words, the members of the New York Stock Exchange) hated, feared, and looked down with condescension on Weeden. After all, this upstart company was stealing business from the good old boys.

I spoke to Fred Siesel, a representative of Weeden, to see if our firms might help one another. Siesel presented me with an offer: Weeden would act as NSI's floor broker on the Pacific exchange to execute in California any order NSI wished. This would mean a great savings for NSI because it would not have to hire anybody to be physically present on the floor of the exchange. NSI would be afforded the use of the Weeden brokers for a 10 percent override on its commissions. For any order NSI received from Tokyo that could be executed in California at the same price as on the New York exchange, NSI would thus keep 90 percent of the commission for itself. The figure could have gone even higher if NSI had only had a better grasp of Wall Street business practices.

In those days, several electronic services were available to execute large stock orders. One was called AutEx and the other Instinet. A subscriber could plug a stock order into the computer, and if another subscriber were interested, contact would be made and the execution completed. NSI's profit potential was unlimited, if it acted like any other American broker. It could go into these systems, or get on the telephone and contact institutions that might wish to buy or sell any of its stocks. Should Nomura find a customer, then Weeden would cross both trades (buy and sell at the same time at the same price) on the Pacific exchange. NSI could double its American commission business, less Weeden's 10 percent.

This approach would also give NSI's trading desk and its institutional sales department far more opportunities to keep in contact with the American institutional investors with something that was of greater immediate interest than Japanese stocks. NSI would be building a name and a reputation to capitalize on when the time came for Americans to start buying Japanese securities. Without a doubt, the financial possibilities were considerable. There was only one hurdle to surmount: Masaaki Kurokawa, senior vice president.

In the fall of 1973, I sat down with NSI's brain trust: Kurokawa; Harunobu Aono, syndicate vice president; Hisaichi Shimizu, head of research; and Vinegar Andy Saitoh, institutional sales department manager. I laid out my idea, expecting to receive hearty congratulations and praise. Instead, Kurokawa summarily rejected my proposal. He huffed that the securities orders coming in from Tokyo were the parent's business, not NSI's. The Pacific Stock Exchange was the concern of NSI's Los Angeles office and of no interest whatsoever to New York.

Those statements didn't add up. At the time, Tokyo handled its business in one of three ways: (1) The parent would channel the order through NSI's trading desk to dole out to any American broker it desired. (2) Tokyo would specify a certain broker that was to get the order. (3) It would bypass NSI and place the order directly with the American broker; NSI never even saw these orders. In most cases NSI had total discretion. Well, why not use that discretion to maximize the firm's income?

Confused and frustrated, I tried to salvage something out of the meeting. I suggested employing the recently acquired seat on the Midwest Stock Exchange instead, thinking that Kuro might take the bait since he was the member of record on that exchange.

That proposal didn't grab him either. He glared stonily at me and said no, turning his back on his own membership. I pleaded my case a bit longer, but it was no use. My proposal to earn hundreds of thousands of dollars for the company was rejected outright. I was shattered. I wondered whether Kuro had any comprehension of what Wall Street was all about.

When I sought commiseration from Riggio, he knitted his brow and asked me, "Was the meeting held in Japanese or in English?"

"It was in English," I said in a deflated voice.

"Well, look at the bright side," he said cheerily. "A great thing was achieved."

"What?" I said, bewildered. "I got turned down."

"It didn't matter," Riggio said. "What was important was, this was the first time that such a high-level meeting had been held in English. It's a breakthrough."

About this time, I cut two gummed labels down to size and stuck them in my dictionary, one over the word *why* and the other so that it blotted out *logic*. After that, I found it a lot easier to deal with NSI.

Some of the goings-on at NSI, however, weren't just mystifying. They were truly worrisome. The first of these transpired one day as I was stationed at my cubbyhole straining to look busy. Yukihiro Terada, the manager of the syndicate department, popped through the door carrying a sheaf of papers, which he proceeded to dump on my desk. I recognized them as order slips, or tickets as we called them. Before I could say anything, Terada said, "Would you please be so kind as to approve orders?"

One of the rules governing the securities business is that all transactions have to be approved by an officer of a brokerage firm. The standard procedure for an order goes like this: The salesperson or trader writes out the ticket and gives it to the order room; an order clerk time-stamps the slip and sends it on to the people who execute it. When the notice of the execution comes back to the clerk, he or she will again time-stamp the original ticket and notify the salesperson. At the end of the day, the sales supervisor and an officer will review all trades to see if there are any irregularities. If none shows up, the officer will initial each ticket.

Even though I was an officer, I was not registered as a principal officer and couldn't approve these trades. What's more, they weren't time-stamped. Time-stamping may sound like no big deal, but it's a vital safeguard for the general public. It prevents someone from being mulcted by a "bucket shop" operator. Bucket shop is slang for a dishonest brokerage firm; they flourished during the 1920s. Before the Rules of Fair Practice of the National Association of Securities Dealers made time-stamping mandatory, a bucket shop would regularly stick a gullible customer with a trade that occurred earlier than the customer's order arrived and at a higher price. Then the bucket shop would pocket the difference. The customer, naturally, would have no way of knowing when the actual trade had taken place.

When I pointed out to Terada that the tickets weren't stamped, he just giggled. Then he hurriedly snatched up the orders, and like a naughty little boy caught dumping a frog in a girl's lunchbox, he scurried across the hall and disappeared. I certainly didn't think NSI was trying to run a modern-day bucket shop. Clearly, it just didn't have a good enough grasp of the rules. But I began to grow uneasy about such troubling oversights.

As time went on and I got more deeply involved in trying to cook up ways to help NSI make more money, I became disturbingly aware of another unusual practice at the firm. NSI violated, again and again, one of the most basic of all securities rules: the requirement that its sales, trading, and supervisory personnel be licensed. In Wall Street jargon, licensing is known as registration. The process is not much different than what a doctor must go through before being allowed to cut out an appendix or work on a prostate. Lawyers have to pass the bar exam before they are permitted to handle divorce cases or defend criminals. You need a license to drive a car, to get married, and to sell stocks and bonds.

All securities that a firm sells must be registered with the SEC before they can legally be marketed in this country. At the same time, in order to conduct business, a brokerage firm, its directors, officers, supervisors, salespeople, traders, and investment bankers all must be registered with the SEC, the National Association of Securities Dealers, various stock exchanges, and/or state governments. Everyone in the securities business in the United States must comply with this basic procedure, even the sleaziest penny-stock operators.

In fact, you hardly ever read in the papers about anyone failing to comply, for the simple reason that it is so rare. About the only notable case to crop up in the last twenty years involved the king of the discount brokers, Charles R. Schwab. In the mid-1980s, before he got into the discount brokerage business, Schwab ran a mutual fund company, and his salespeople sold shares of a Schwab-managed mutual fund throughout the country, including Texas. That was where the trouble lay. The fund wasn't registered with the state's securities division. When the authorities got wind of this, securities regulators came down on the fund, and it is now defunct. The officers were lucky they didn't get thrown in jail. In New York State, they could have been imprisoned for up to a year and barred from the securities business. Obviously, registration is nothing to take lightly.

Becoming registered to sell stocks is much harder than getting your driver's license. Prospective brokers spend up to six months, and their firms spend from $6,000 to $60,000 per trainee, preparing for the stringent written examination known as Series 7. And many fail. Supervisors must pass a still tougher test called Series 8, and Wall Street officers and corporate directors are required to take a mind-bender called Series 24.

Up until now, my experience had always been that virtually everyone complied. Everyone, apparently, except NSI. It had a decidedly different tack on this. While working in institutional sales and in the syndicate department, I really had no idea whether the newly arrived Japanese salesmen who had just hopped off the red-eye from Tokyo were properly licensed by the American authorities to conduct securities business. Nor was I in any position to know whether the Japanese supervisors were registered. Wall Street people, unlike cab drivers, don't have to display their licenses for all to see. But I had a gut feeling that these guys were operating on the sly. How could they be registered? They couldn't really speak English, couldn't understand English, and certainly didn't comprehend the American brokerage business. So how could they possibly pass a written examination?

In time, I learned the answer. They couldn't and hadn't. To be fair, most NSI people would eventually become licensed, though often years after they began selling securities. But a few supervisors didn't bother to become licensed at all. As I came to find out, NSI's failure to register its personnel began in the early 1970s. When Lou Riggio came on board in 1970, he was already licensed as a registered representative with the National Association of Securities Dealers, the New York Stock Exchange, and several states, including New York. About a year later, Yoshio Terasawa, NSI's president, asked Riggio to take the NASD registered principal's examination that was required for brokerage firm officials. He did, and he passed.

So Riggio was all set. When NSI bought a seat on the Pacific Stock Exchange in 1971, however, it became necessary for all of the company's pertinent employees to satisfy the PSE's licensing requirements. At first, the New York City staff felt no need to comply. The New York people insisted that it was the business of the Los Angeles office. The Japanese, you see, saw no relationship between two offices within NSI. They considered themselves employees of the parent, and the various American locations nothing more than branch offices within the Nomura system. Thus, as far as it was concerned, the New York office had nothing to do with the Los Angeles office. What's more, the Japanese are no different from anyone else when it comes to filling out forms. They'd rather fight a bout of the flu. But the PSE required papers to be filed. Finally, NSI's management decided to ease the burden by circulating a copy of Riggio's registration form for the staff to follow. Everyone did.

Once the forms were completed, it was Riggio's job to collect them and forward them to the PSE. Fortunately, he had the good sense to check the applications before he sent them. It turned out that everybody had been born in 1938 in New York City, they had all graduated from Yale in 1959, they had all served in the U.S. Marine Corps (some feat for the Japanese), and they had all been employed by the American Foreign Service before they all joined Harris Upham!

Others at NSI just never got around to registering at all. They sold stocks, underwrote new issues, traded, all without a license. I actually later came to be in charge of registrations at NSI, though I was instructed that I would be responsible for the registrations of only the American staff in the New York office. I was told the Japanese staff would take care of the Tokyo people. I could see why.

The only known attempt on the part of the NASD, or any regulatory agency for that matter, to make NSI comply with licensing requirements was on March 18, 1975, when the NASD sent a letter on the subject to NSI's law firm, Kelley Drye & Warren. A courtesy copy was sent to Terasawa. The letter was pretty tough, and it zeroed in on several of NSI's senior officers and directors. The most important were Hideo Suzuki, Kiyoshi Kobayashi, and Masayuki Iwai. The first was NSI's then chairman, and the other two were senior vice presidents and members of the board of directors. No lightweights there. The letter ordered Kobayashi and Iwai "not [to] function in the capacity designated [department supervisors] . . . until . . . qualified by examination."

The letter noted that Suzuki was in Tokyo and didn't fall under the registration requirements, but an exemption request had not yet been filed. Then it picked up on Kobayashi. It noted his application for examination had been pending since April 18, 1974, almost a year, overlooking the fact that he had been working at NSI for five months before he even bothered to submit an application. Another four months would dribble by before Kobayashi passed the registered principal test on July 15, 1975. So he managed to serve a full twenty months as a member of NSI's senior management without being licensed.

Iwai was in charge of the trading department and supervised the day-to-day operations of its desk for nine months before being spotted by the NASD. Another eight months were to go by before he passed the required examination. All told, he was unlicensed for seventeen months.

These were the only offenses the NASD caught, and the agency must have looked the other way. It did nothing to enforce its rules beyond that one letter. As far as I could tell, NSI's law firm never brought any pressure either. Judging by Kobayshi's and Iwai's lack of compliance with the NASD order, it was business as usual at NSI: All ignored the NASD directive, and NSI merrily continued to violate the rules.

6

The 100,000-Share Order

O NE SLOW MORNING, TERASAWA'S SECRETARY AP-
proached me and asked if I had anything special to do that
afternoon. I shrugged and said, "Nothing that couldn't wait."
In that case, she said, could I meet Terasawa at two o'clock on
the twenty-fifth floor of the General Motors Building on Fifth
Avenue across from the Plaza Hotel?

I hadn't any idea what all this was about, and since Miss
Murata didn't have any details either, I merely acquiesced and
returned to what I was doing.

When I got off the elevator at the appointed time, I was
greeted by Terry and two representatives from Morgan Stanley. There was the usual cordial exchange, and then David
Collier, GM's treasurer, materialized out of nowhere and beckoned us into a mammoth conference room done up in mahogany.

One of the Morgan men cleared his throat and opened the
meeting with some remarks about listing General Motors' stock
on the Tokyo Stock Exchange. So this was what the meeting
was about. Why I was here, however, was still a complete
puzzle. I didn't know a blessed thing about listing stocks on the
Tokyo market. I wasn't even sure in which part of town the
Tokyo exchange was located.

Morgan Stanley was GM's American investment banker,
which is why it was at the meeting, and I guessed that GM
needed Nomura's expertise in Japan. Once Morgan was done,
the meeting evolved into a two-way discussion between Collier
and Terasawa. As they chattered on, Collier asked so many

questions that it was as if Terry were confronting a panel on "Face the Nation."

From what I could tell, Terry gave a remarkable accounting of himself. Every question was fielded deftly and answered to the apparent satisfaction of GM's treasurer. Before it ended, the conversation had moved into rarefied heights that were well beyond my understanding. And judging from the faces of the Morgan Stanley people, beyond theirs, too. I know I would have been hopelessly lost if I had been called upon to answer. I was duly impressed.

Once the meeting wrapped up, Collier gave us all a brief tour of the floor, and then we went our separate ways. As I rode downtown with Terry, he turned to me and explained why I had been summoned to the meeting. He had been told that two people from Morgan Stanley would be attending, so he felt it only proper that two Nomura people be there as well. He had sent his secretary scurrying around the office looking for a body, and I was the only warm one she could find who was available.

Terry then leaned over and asked, "When Mr. Collier said [and he rattled off some question that had been asked], what did he mean?"

I looked at him, astonished. Then I explained the meaning of the question.

He breathed a sigh of relief. "I gave the right answer," he said.

Then Terry repeated another of Collier's questions and asked me what that one meant. When I told him, he sighed again and repeated, "I gave him the right answer."

I was stunned. Terry actually was not even sure of what he was being asked at the meeting and had winged it with his answers hoping to guess right. You might call that salesmanship of the highest order, but it also caused me to wonder seriously about the qualifications of my bosses and the way they did business.

Every stockbroker dreams of someday receiving an order for a hundred thousand shares. It is a magic number that few ever hear, though most would gladly shake hands with the Devil for the privilege. Dumb luck, though, can strike anybody once.

Here's how I got my own hundred-thousand-share order—and why I didn't celebrate.

Every morning I sat and listened with bemusement to my two fellow salesmen in the institutional sales department, Naomichi Shimao and Hiroshi Kawanaka, as they made their morning calls to prospective customers. They would begin by listing the highlights of what had happened on the Tokyo Stock Exchange, then comment on any economic developments of consequence that might affect the markets. So far, so good. Then the following would inevitably happen.

They would tell the customer, "Today Tokyo is a seller of hundred thousand shares of XYZ" — "XYZ" being whatever Japanese company was on NSI's daily disposal list of stocks to sell. "So do you want to buy a hundred shares of XYZ?"

The reply, naturally, was a flat no. The salesman's voice would shoot up an octave or two as he said, in a rapid-fire delivery, "Whaaaat? You don't want to buy a hundred shares of XYZ . . . Oh, not on approved rist."

And then it was merrily on to the next call and the same dialogue. It was pitiful. Tens of millions of dollars passed through the telephones of the crack salesmen on Wall Street. At NSI, we were talking about a buck-fifty. At first, I found these pitches pretty funny—I mean, who in the world could sell anything that way—but after I heard them an interminable number of times, they became depressing.

For a long time, I didn't butt in. After all, even though there were just the four of us, my Japanese colleagues rarely had all that much to do with me. My isolation was in part dictated by the fact that I didn't speak Japanese, and my coworkers weren't much into talking English. What's more, they were ten or fifteen years younger and, like the other Nomura men, favored frequenting Japanese piano bars after work and hunting for "entertainment ladies." Neither my age nor my wife would have gone along with that pursuit, assuming I were ever asked along. I wasn't. Shimao was certainly nice enough to me. He always had a smile on his face and a twinkle in his eyes behind his gold-rimmed glasses. He was quick to giggle. But he never did look on me as one of the boys. With Kawanaka, there was the additional problem that he disliked Americans. He was polite, all right, but he almost never engaged me in any conversation. Since I was a Nomura employee, I suppose he felt obliged to tolerate me, and that he did. I was essentially regarded as the equivalent of a chair or a floor lamp.

Before long, I found it sad watching the guys smash into a stone wall day after day. They simply couldn't learn anything from their mistakes. You would think that the Japanese, hungry as they were to make their presence felt in this country, would be synthesizing the skills and procedures of American salespeople. But they weren't. They were like robots that had been programmed to speak Russian and then mistakenly shipped to China. I finally mustered up the courage to do something.

I started off by trying to tell Kurokawa, Harunobo Aono, the syndicate vice president, and Vinegar Andy that the sales approach was maybe not the most effective one that could be devised. But none of them would listen. Even that luncheon with the people from Kansas City Securities had made no impression. The fruitless routine went on and on.

Finally, Kuro came over to me one day and issued a challenge: "You get an order for a hundred thousand shares, I will listen."

"But all buyers of Japanese stocks are covered by someone at NSI, and I would be stepping into their territory," I said. "And what kind of trading and research backup can I get from the parent?"

"I give you permission to call on anybody," Kuro said. "That is the support you need."

Great! I thought.

But there's nothing easy about getting a hundred-thousand-share order. If there had been, there would have been no need for me to open my mouth. In all, it took me a good year and a half after that conversation to nail one. And things didn't exactly transpire the way I had envisioned.

One day Timothy Price, a representative from Howard, Weil, Labouisse, Fredrichs, Inc., of New Orleans visited our offices. Since NSI regarded the firm as small and trivial, none of the Japanese wanted to be bothered, and so I was assigned to meet with him. Price was a solid professional. The firm was developing its international business, and since Japan was starting to open up, it wanted to get to know Nomura.

Nothing much happened at that session, but meeting Price proved fortuitous. About a year later, Price left Howard, Weil to form his own investment company. It was set up in the Bahamas but managed out of New Orleans. Shortly after opening up shop, Price decided he wanted to sink some money into the Japanese stock market, but he didn't know any of NSI's salesmen. He called the only person he had ever met at the firm: me.

By this time, I had been transferred to the corporate syndicate department, where I was underwriting American stocks and bonds and had nothing to do with selling Japanese stocks. Nevertheless, I listened to Price, opened an account, and took his order. I had to catch my breath when I heard what it was: a hundred thousand shares of Kirin Brewery. Bingo, I had gotten the magic order.

I excitedly placed the order with NSI's trading desk. Then the nightmare began.

NSI was a market maker in Kirin Brewery in New York. This meant it was an over-the-counter dealer that bought and sold shares for its own account from anybody who wanted to trade the stock. Because Kirin was traded on the Tokyo Stock Exchange, NSI was not a dealer in its actual common stock but in its American Depository Receipts. ADRs are issued by American banks that hold the actual foreign shares on deposit. The receipts are essentially facsimiles for the real shares, and the American investor can buy and sell them in the United States without having to place orders in the foreign stock markets. Because of the thirteen-hour time difference between Tokyo and New York, U.S.–originated transactions in Japanese stocks can be confusing and chancy. It's nearly impossible to know the condition of the market before an order is placed, and it takes a full day to get back a report of a completed transaction.

With Kirin Brewery, one ADR represented ten Japanese shares. When Price gave me his order, an ADR was quoted at $9 bid, $9.25 offered. In other words, NSI would be willing to buy the ADR at $9 and sell it at $9.25.

Price would have been perfectly happy to accept that figure. He wasn't shopping around for bargains. But the trading department cooked up a slightly different proposition. It gave Price a choice. NSI would execute the hundred thousand shares in Tokyo the next day at whatever price it could get and charge him a standard commission. Or the desk would give him the opportunity to buy ten thousand ADRs at the unheard-of price of $9 a share. That was a stupendous bargain, because Price would have had to pay at least $9.25 or more for an order of that magnitude. What's more, the $9 price would be without a commission.

No one in his right mind would refuse an offer like that. Being in his right mind, Price jumped at the deal. He liked picking money up off the floor as much as the next guy.

NSI didn't actually have the ADRs to sell Price. It had "shorted" the stock to the buyer, a common technique on Wall Street. Of course, to have something to deliver to the client, the dealer must either borrow the shares or buy the stock, hopefully at a lower price than it was selling for when the client placed the order. The trading desk in New York thought it could buy the Japanese common stock more cheaply on the Tokyo Stock Exchange the next day, convert it into the ADRs, and deliver them to Price, filling the order and maybe making a little profit on the side.

Alas, things didn't quite work out that way. Either Tim Price knew something NSI didn't, or he got awfully lucky. The next day, the shares of Kirin Brewery soared on the Tokyo Stock Exchange. As a result, NSI suddenly had a very expensive problem on its hands.

Of course, neither Price nor I knew that NSI had shorted the ADRs. After the transaction was paid for, I decided it was finally time to step up and be counted for my hundred-thousand-share order. Then Kurokawa would have to listen to my sage advice on how to sell stocks to institutions in the United States. Once the advice was followed, I would no doubt be promoted to the presidency of NSI and paid a zillion dollars a year.

Before I was able to blurt out the news, my boss in the syndicate department stopped me. "Big trouble," he said in a hushed voice. "The trading department made mistake. Big mistake."

He wasn't kidding. I found out that the desk had to buy the shares in Japan at a price equal to between $10.25 and $10.75 per ADR. The order, therefore, had lost the company more than $10,000, then a record loss for any single securities transaction at NSI. Kurokawa was waiting with a short fuse for the person responsible for placing the order to come forward and take credit. It didn't seem to matter to him that it was the trading desk that had blown it; I suppose he reasoned that if the order had never come in, then the trading desk couldn't very well have screwed up.

I decided I could live without the honor. So I meekly went about my business in the syndicate department, underwriting stocks and bonds, and left it to the institutional sales force to chase after future hundred-thousand-share orders. It's funny how a hero at Nomura can almost simultaneously become a scapegoat.

7

Midwest, Here We Come

IN THEIR AIM TO GAIN DOMINION OVER NEW TERRITORIES, the Japanese brokerage firms that set up affiliates in this country targeted four areas: investment, securities research, underwriting, and trading. There was enough desire in the air to make for some spicy doings in all four of these, though progress came haltingly. In the fall of 1973, to justify my existence a little, I helped hatch a plan with the Midwest Stock Exchange that would enable NSI to take a big step forward in trading. At the time, the company didn't really have a clue about what it was being steered into, but the plan would mean that NSI could become the first Japanese specialist on any American securities exchange, which would elevate it to an enviable leadership role among the Japanese firms.

By late in 1973 the Japanese Ministry of Finance had relaxed its rules governing the execution of American stocks so that the Japanese were no longer restricted to the New York Stock Exchange and could trade on other exchanges. In those days, most of NSI's American securities orders came from Japan, but on rare occasions orders came from U.S. institutional investors who were compensating NSI for securities research it was providing in Japanese equities. Even though hardly any investing was being done in Japan, there was the future to look to. The institutions felt it was prudent to get acquainted with the largest securities market outside the United States. The market value of shares traded on the Tokyo Stock Exchange was only half that of the New York Stock Exchange, but it was still three times greater than on the London Exchange. So it would have been foolhardy to completely close your eyes to what was going on in Tokyo.

One of the institutions that kept a watch on the market was the Chase Manhattan Bank. As the largest Japanese broker, Nomura was automatically added to Chase's list of approved securities firms. Accordingly, the bank's trading department was under instructions to feed NSI a certain amount of commission business.

Chase's head trader at the time, Bernie Joyce, very much preferred to satisfy these orders by doing underwriting transactions with NSI's syndicate department rather than by getting mixed up with our stock-trading desk. To give a broker commissions in underwritings was a relatively simple procedure. All the bank had to do was tell the American underwriter to allocate shares or bonds to NSI, and the underwriting firm would do so. The price of any underwriting was fixed, and so were the commissions. The execution of the orders and delivery of the securities were handled by the American firm. All NSI had to do was to lean back with its feet up and collect its underwriting commissions. It was a fail-safe system.

I used to call Joyce regularly to fill him in on what NSI was underwriting. If Chase liked something, the system described above would be set into motion. But Joyce said that buying American stocks through NSI was totally chaotic. The mere thought of giving NSI a stock order made him cringe because he would be forced to deal with either some young, fast-talking, big-mouthed American kid at NSI who was still learning the ropes, or some Japanese who couldn't speak or understand any English. It was Joyce's job to get the best execution for the Chase Bank, not to be a training program for NSI's young American traders or an English teacher for its Tokyo staff. So Joyce always chose underwritings as the way to pay NSI its commissions.

This got me to thinking. If we were going to start making big money, we had to learn to trade stocks smoothly so Chase and the other institutions would use us. After Kurokawa rejected my proposal to execute Tokyo's block trades through Weeden on the Pacific Stock Exchange, Riggio and I decided to appeal to outside help to try to get something going. The man we approached was Sandy Thomas. With his blond hair and blue eyes, Claude "Sandy" Thomas could have easily become a professional model, but had instead settled for working for the Midwest Stock Exchange as its senior representative in the New York City area. His job was to cultivate interest in the Midwest operation, no easy assignment when you're playing in the backyard of both the New York and American stock exchanges. Thomas set out to make himself known to the Midwest exchange's newest member, and thus he became fairly chummy with Lou and me. Naturally, he was keen for NSI to make full use of the services of the Midwest exchange.

Thomas made several approaches to NSI's management on the subject and, in the end, didn't get a millimeter further than I did. When Thomas showed Aono a list of large trades (stock orders of more than ten thousand shares) that had been executed on the Midwest exchange, Aono spotted one of NSI's that had been given to an American broker for execution in Chicago. It was for ten thousand shares of some stock selling for about $30 a share. Aono told Thomas: "There's one of our orders!" The fact that NSI could have done the trade itself on the Midwest exchange made no impression whatsoever on Aono, nor on anyone else at NSI.

I discovered that if the Japanese don't understand something in a foreign market, they simply ignore it. If they do comprehend it but it doesn't fit into Japanese business methods, then it might be followed for a short time before being abandoned. This attitude might explain why it took Nomura so long to penetrate the American financial markets. It had all the tools it needed and should have done so long before.

In November 1973 the company had a happy accident that moved it a big step further along the road. On November 26, a Monday, Sandy Thomas called to tell me that Laurence Barr, the executive vice president of the Midwest Stock Exchange, would be in New York on Wednesday. There was an opening in his schedule at three P.M. Would NSI be interested? I said we sure would.

Now I had two problems: First, how was I going to inform Kurokawa, and second, how was I going to lure him into the meeting?

Fortunately, Kurokawa was out of the office when Thomas called; otherwise he would have waved off the invitation on the spot. I decided to write him a memo telling him about the telephone call and reporting that I had confirmed the meeting. Since Kuro had no real interest in the Midwest Stock Exchange, he only glanced at the note and handed it to his assistant, Hisaichi Shimizu.

Shimizu was Kuro's right-hand man, besides being vice president in charge of NSI's Japanese securities research. That was his official function, at least. In practice, his primary job was to think up new and ingenious ways to lose at mah-jongg to Kuro. Kuro, you see, was known as the best mah-jongg player of the Japanese nationals assigned to New York. Even on an off day, he would whip all comers. Or at least he would appear to thrash them. The thing is, underlings were not supposed to make their superiors look bad, so I could never be altogether sure just how handy Kuro was with those tiles. But the fact that he routinely pocketed all the wagers might partly explain why the pay scale of the Tokyo staff was nearly 50 to 100 percent higher than that of the Americans who were doing the same or equivalent jobs. They had phenomenal gambling debts to pay off to the senior vice president.

Shimizu, who had even less interest in the Midwest Stock Exchange than Kuro, handed the memo back to me. It took less time for this scrap of paper to be passed from me to Kuro to Shimizu and then back to me than it takes for a baseball to make its way around the Mets infield. The ball was back in my hands.

On that Wednesday, Sandy Thomas, Larry Barr, and a Japanese female translator arrived at three o'clock sharp. They were ushered into the chairman's office, and I informed Kuro that they were waiting.

Kuro arched an eyebrow and asked, "A Japanese girl, too?"

"Yes, a Japanese girl," I replied. "I know a girl when I see one."

"I hope so," Kuro said.

The presence of a Japanese female on the premises changed everything. You could feel the electric charge in the air. Now, nothing could keep NSI's management out of the meeting. In scampered Mutt and Jeff, with Shimizu practically stepping on their heels.

Barr, all business, told them of the manifold benefits open to the members of the Midwest Stock Exchange, including the possibility of being a specialist, or dealer, on the exchange.

This is a key position of trust in any securities market. Basically, a specialist legally manipulates the stocks assigned to him or her, and must maintain an inventory of these stocks. If an excess of buyers comes charging into the market, the specialist must sell them stock from that inventory to curb the wave of buying. When sellers stampede to dump their shares, the specialist has to buy for his or her inventory. This is called "maintaining an orderly market." Without such risk-takers, the stock markets would deteriorate into total chaos. More often than not, besides serving a vital function, a specialist can make an enormous profit. But if a specialist's luck turns bad, a small fortune can vanish in a flash.

Barr discussed many other things, and the role of the specialist drew no more attention. Barr did say that a European specialist member was bidding on several stocks that were becoming available at week's end. Barr felt that becoming a specialist on the MSE might be something worthwhile for NSI's future and suggested we consider such a move, either then or at a later date.

At the moment, it was awfully tough for my Japanese colleagues to consider much of anything. Although they periodically smiled at Barr in a placatory way, Barr's comments were lost on them. They were much more interested in the female translator than in the business of the Midwest Stock Exchange. For much of the meeting, they sat peeking out of the corner of their eyes at her. From what I could tell, she ignored the vibes.

Fortunately for NSI, I kept my eyes on Larry Barr and listened to what was being said. The meeting lasted about forty-five minutes, and then everybody went back to business. I got no feedback whatsoever from NSI's management. But on Friday I heard from the Midwest exchange.

Barr telephoned to tell me that one of the stocks that was going up for bids for a new specialist was Sony. He wanted to advise NSI of the latest development because Nomura was Sony's investment banker in Japan and had comanaged its initial American stock offering in 1962. Barr also cautioned that it might be a little late for NSI to step into the bidding competition, so time was of the essence.

I thanked him and said we would get right back to him. After I hung up, I told Kurokawa about the coming change of specialist. Finally, Kuro showed a glimmer of interest.

Kuro asked if it was an American company or a Japanese firm bidding for the Sony job. I told him it was a foreign firm, but the exchange wouldn't be any more specific. That woke him up like a bomb. Panic filled the air.

Had Kuro paid the slightest bit of attention to Larry Barr, he would have surmised that it was a European broker competing for the position. Kuro felt that it would not be a problem if someone else took over the Sony book, but it would be a major disaster for Nomura if it were another Japanese broker. NSI couldn't possibly allow that to happen. Because they had been so transfixed by the female translator, however, they had missed what was being said.

Now NSI jumped into the bidding for Sony with both feet. It put a bid on the table of the exchange a few minutes before the five o'clock deadline on Friday.

Later, Barr told me the real story. The Midwest Stock Exchange badly wanted to get Nomura involved, and it thought the role of a specialist in Sony would be a good start. Thus, no matter what happened, the exchange was going to see to it that Nomura was named the Sony specialist (the exchange had the final word in the specialist selection), but it let NSI worry for a few days. It figured that if the process were made to look too easy, Nomura wouldn't take it seriously.

Once NSI was declared the winner, it still had a slight problem. It didn't have a person working on the floor of the Midwest exchange, which was a requirement for a specialist. Again, Larry Barr came to the rescue. He approached the largest specialist on the exchange, A. G. Becker, and asked if the firm would be willing to act as a specialist's agent for another member. Reluctantly, Becker agreed.

On December 10 the advertisement announcing that Nomura had been awarded the specialist book for Sony appeared in the *Wall Street Journal*. That's when NSI almost lost the assignment.

For many years, the Boston Stock Exchange specialist Cantella & Company had handled the Sony book in Boston. It had once had a congenial working relationship with NSI. As NSI started to expand and new people came into place, however, the two firms drifted apart. By this time, neither was any longer in touch with the other. Those of us who had been involved in NSI's bid to become a specialist didn't know about the old Cantella relationship. Lou Riggio was aware of it, but matters had moved too speedily for him to give thought to the Boston specialist.

The *Wall Street Journal* ad set off some fireworks in Boston. The Cantella people felt horribly betrayed, since nobody from NSI had contacted them about the move. They made their feelings explicitly known to Terasawa, NSI's president, and were invited to come to New York to talk over the situation.

Two days later, Vincent Cantella and Edmond Ryan, Jr., arrived for their meeting with NSI. Since they had a complaint that might cause the meeting to get unpleasant, the Japanese didn't attend. Riggio was nominated, along with Terasawa's new American assistant, a man I'll call Ben Goodly.

The inimitable Ben Goodly was destined to play a significant role in Nomura's future. Goodly grew up in Chicago and served as an officer in the navy in World War II, though he never had too much to say about his war experiences. After all, a Japanese company wasn't the greatest place to tell heroic World War II stories. Goodly had extremely bushy eyebrows that made you forget about his receding hairline. His mouth was usually half-open and his brow knitted. It gave you the distinct impression you weren't making yourself understood when speaking to him. In my estimation, the most valuable asset Goodly brought to Nomura was a top-notch golf game. He regularly shot in the mid to high seventies. And there were few things the Japanese appreciated more than a crackerjack golf game.

Goodly had been a partner at a small stock brokerage firm in Chicago until it was taken over by the now-defunct Walston & Company and Goodly moved to New York to be with his new partners. Goodly was a man with capital, and in the twenty-five years that followed World War II, that was all one needed to prosper on Wall Street. Starting in the late 1960s, however, Wall Street witnessed the decline and fall of many brokerage firms as the old school ties, the private New York clubs, and the personal wealth of the partners succumbed to the professionals and the huge pools of capital of the publicly owned corporations.

In 1973 H. Ross Perot added Walston & Company to his huge stable. One of the first moves that Perot is said to have made upon acquiring Walston was to personally dismiss Ben Goodly. At least that was the way Goodly told it, as if this were some badge of honor. Goodly was out of work from July until October 1973, when Terasawa hired him.

When Riggio learned there was a new presidential assistant, he asked Terry why he had chosen Goodly. Terry told Riggio that he had been approached by two of Wall Street's exalted figures. Both were managing partners of their firms, which were among the giants of the brokerage industry. They told Terasawa that what he needed to further NSI's position in the American financial marketplace was a top guy who was well known and respected on Wall Street. Ben Goodly, they said, was such a man. Terry bought the story without blinking.

(Thirteen years later, in 1986, Terasawa was to give the same explanation when James Needham, the former president of the New York Stock Exchange, was hired as a consultant to NSI. Déjà vu time.)

Riggio asked Terry why, if Goodly was such a high-powered person, one of the two other firms didn't hire him. At such large firms, there's always room for talent.

Terry said Goodly was too old.

Well, then, why wasn't he too old for NSI?

Terry simply put his hands up, covered his face, and said nothing.

Before the meeting with the Cantella people, Riggio asked me to speak to Goodly, because I had had many discussions with the Midwest Stock Exchange and knew the lay of the land. I took Goodly aside to brief him on what to say and not to say. The Midwest people had warned me about some of the pitfalls of the new position. The most important consideration was to avoid setting up a joint book of operations with another specialist firm, especially if that firm was also a member of the New York Stock Exchange. The New York exchange had a rule covering joint books for its members on another exchange, and it was strictly enforced. The rule specified that all orders for any stock traded on the New York exchange must first be sent to its floor for execution. If the order couldn't be done, then, and only then, it could be sent to another stock exchange.

Thus, should NSI enter into a joint-book operation with any NYSE member, NSI's specialist operation would be placed under the NYSE rules, and it would probably never have an opportunity to act as the specialist for Sony on the Midwest exchange. All orders would have to be funneled to the NYSE. And Cantella was a NYSE member firm.

I explained a few other things to Goodly, but this was the most important one, and I stressed: "No joint specialist, or Nomura will lose everything."

Bewilderment swept across Goodly's face. His eyes glazed over and turned blank. As I stared at his half-opened mouth, I had the uncomfortable feeling I wasn't getting through to NSI's presidential advisor.

The meeting lasted more than an hour, and during it Riggio kept stepping out to consult with me about certain items. There must have been more than a hundred people who knew more than I did on this topic, but none was at NSI, and the management had not asked me to attend the meeting. That was standard procedure at NSI.

Finally, Riggio came dashing out and asked me about NSI and Cantella getting together to form a joint specialist operation.

I gnashed my teeth. I was livid. I gave a one-word answer, "Don't."

Then he said, "Ben just committed Nomura to a joint book on Sony with Cantella."

Less than forty-five minutes had passed since I told Goodly that such a move would be disastrous. Yet the guy made the move! Out of desperation, Riggio broke all the rules and asked me into the meeting. Quickly, I withdrew Goodly's offer. I explained NSI's situation, and Vinny Cantella grudgingly agreed with our position. If NSI linked itself with an NYSE member, then most if not all of our Sony business would go through the NYSE rather than the Midwest exchange. That was the rule, and Cantella knew the rules, though he very much wanted to gain a stronger relationship with NSI.

To show there were no hard feelings, Cantella took everybody out to lunch. During the luncheon Cantella finally told us what had angered him; nobody from NSI had the simple courtesy to inform his company about the pending move. He was right about that. Somebody should have.

Once all that was settled, we got our operation going. As it turned out, the first month on the Midwest exchange, with A. G. Becker calling the shots for NSI on the specialist operation, we lost money, an occupational hazard. Then NSI's head trader, Masaharu "Mark" Izumi, took charge and transformed the operation into a gold mine. Izumi was one of the few quality people Tokyo transferred overseas. He was a true professional, and so long as Izumi remained with NSI, it never had another losing month. He was transferred to London in 1977 and soon afterward became one of the first Japanese to bolt Nomura for a better job.

From this modest beginning, NSI steadily built up its American trading capabilities. Because of Izumi's success in handling the Sony specialist's book, the Midwest exchange assigned additional securities to NSI. Within a few short years, it expanded its specialist operations to more than a dozen stocks and became a factor to be reckoned with in the American marketplace.

(In the mid-1980s, NSI changed its policy, and instead of hiring inexperienced Americans, it began to lure American professionals from their U.S. companies by waving sizable salaries under their noses. By the summer of 1988, when it was a New York Stock Exchange member, NSI accounted for nearly 10 percent of the exchange's volume. It was not, however, due to savvy trading. Tokyo discovered "dividend rollovers." This is a tactic whereby investors buy shares of a company the day before it is due to pay a dividend and then dump the stock the following day. The objective is to capture the dividend for tax purposes. Although there is nothing illegal about the maneuver, the Japanese Ministry of Finance put a halt to the practice the next year. Subsequently NSI became a factor in "program trading," in which sophisticated computer programs dictate which stocks to buy and sell.)

Several years later, I told my superior, Yukihiro Terada, by then the chief of the syndicate department, the story of my involvement in Nomura's highly profitable Midwest Stock Exchange specialist operation. Terada apparently broached the subject at a Japanese staff meeting, because he came roaring out of the meeting and yanked me aside. He was pretty rattled and said, breathlessly, "Fitz-san, you had nothing to do with the Midwest Stock Exchange specialist role. Nothing at all. It was all Kuro-san's doing! Kuro-san said he did everything; you had no involvement."

8

Sell, Sell, Sell

As I watched the Nomura people scurrying around the financial landscape like an army of ants, crawling in and out of underbrush looking for something juicy to nibble on, I tried to make some sense of what I was seeing. By now, I had been at NSI for about a year, long enough to obtain a reasonable understanding of the peculiar personnel policies and pecking order of the company. They are worth some elaboration because they are illustrative not only of Nomura but of the way the Japanese mind works, especially in business.

The clearest rule was that the Japanese-Japanese from Tokyo were considered permanent employees and a protected species. Everyone else was looked upon as temporary, someone who might be around for a few years, a few months, or a few minutes. The Tokyo people were relentless cheerleaders, who always carried the company flag around with them and proudly wore their Nomura logo pins on the lapels of their suits. The rest of us didn't, for company pins were never issued to the local staff. Anyone not within the mainstream of the parent wasn't considered a true member of the company, but something akin to rented furniture. To be one of the brethren, one had to be a male Japanese national hired in Japan.

Even the handful of Japanese-American nisei, I found out, were treated as second-class citizens, if not third-class. The Japanese looked upon the nisei as American and therefore deemed them *gaijin*. I knew of some Japanese companies where the Japanese-Americans actually encountered harsher treatment than any other ethnic group. Apparently, they were considered cultural throwbacks.

Within Nomura, there were basically two types of permanent employees (forgetting females, who never counted to the Japanese). The male college graduate was considered "professional" and managerial material. The high school graduate was relegated to the company's clerical ranks. The former had a shot at making it into the company's senior management ranks; the latter didn't.

Much has been written about how the productivity of the Japanese is so much higher than the Americans', and there is certainly truth in the statement. However, there is an underlying difference between the corporate systems. The basic feeling among the Japanese employees is that they own the company de facto, and it exists for their sole benefit. They are accountable only to themselves for the existence and (but not always) for the betterment of the company. It is the difference between owning and renting a house. The Japanese are willing to put in the extra hours to mow the lawn and clean the gutters.

Because of this attitude, the average Japanese professional develops much greater flexibility during his career than the American. Accordingly, he has no strong feelings about being transferred from job to job, department to department, location to location, and even from Japan to another country. Most Japanese are generalists. Ideally, they know their company and every one of its facets.

Up to a point, the Japanese professional will be promoted routinely in accordance with the year he joined the company. This approach is almost exactly like that of the U.S. military academies, where each class progresses through the lower and middle ranks on a fixed time schedule and together.

Another difference between the American and the Japanese concerns individual rewards and recognitions for a job well done. An American expects his or her contributions to be reflected in a bigger paycheck. A Japanese employee is assigned greater duties and responsibilities with no pay increase.

A foreign assignment to a Japanese worker, however, is not necessarily a positive career development. It removes him from his intraoffice political circle. It is critical for him to maintain these contacts if he wants to ascend the ladder, and a move overseas cuts him off. The isolation from family and friends is always regarded as a much lesser factor, more an inconvenience than an actual drawback. Even if a person wretchedly missed his family, he would rarely admit it; that's just not the Japanese style. ("How are the wife and kids? Oh, all right. Haven't seen them in two years.")

The corporate decision-making at NSI generally came from within the company and not from senior management. Somehow an idea would find its way into the company's maze and work its way up the ranks to senior management, whose approval usually was perfunctory. Before anything could become company policy, therefore, it had to be thoroughly discussed and harmonized. If one person wasn't in agreement, the proposal would languish. This did not mean it was dead. It might float around for a while until everyone came back to it. If pushed for an answer, however, it would be no. This didn't necessarily mean the proposal had no merit; it simply meant the group couldn't reach complete harmony, and so it gave a thumbs-down by default. However, once everybody agreed, the proposal would be acted upon with the speed of summer lightning before anybody could change his mind.

One thing that was always clear, to Japanese and *gaijin* alike, was that all the real decisions were reached in Tokyo. Nobody at the local level had any actual voice in NSI's overall corporate policies. The *gaijin*, however, had the toughest time even knowing what was going on. Because xenophobia is deep-seated in the Japanese, the local *gaijin* were rarely included in any important meetings and never consulted in matters relating to corporate politics. The Tokyo people would pass along only what they considered "need-to-know" information to the in-house non-Japanese. We would never get the complete story or proper facts, only bits and pieces. However, the Japanese had little understanding or knowledge of the local marketplace, customs, and rules and regulations governing the markets. Therefore they were in no position to correctly evaluate and identify the real "need-to-know" items. Usually what was passed along was worthless, about as helpful as the previous day's weather forecast. It only added to the confusion and generally fanned the flames of distrust on both sides.

Another curious side to the overseas Japanese manager was

the transformation in his personality. Because Japanese society is group-oriented, once an individual is removed from his protective pocket, he has no guidelines on how to interface with others in the new environment. Sometimes the supervisor of an overseas operation would be given a free hand to pursue the parent's goals. As a rule, however, there was nothing in the manager's background to prepare him for his new overseas assignment. He neither could nor would turn to his subordinates, and he did not trust his local employees; he was very much on his own. As a result, there was no way for him to get a consensus among his peers for guidance. Tokyo didn't really care. It was interested only in market penetration, not how it was achieved.

More often than not, these international managers were not the company's plums. The road to the company's presidency led through the national side, not international operations. Therefore the best people never worked a day outside Japan.

That was why the international executives of the Japanese companies were generally sneered at by their peers in Japan. It was assumed that if they had any smarts, they would be needed in the more important areas of the company's business—and overseas wasn't as important as Americans are given to think. The Tokyo-based executives claimed the only thing the overseas people could do was "speak English." This was the ultimate put-down and meant the international people knew nothing about business. Of course, there were exceptions to the rule, but not too many.

The truth was, the local staffers at NSI were considered "temporary" despite their titles, their positions, and their length of service. The professional *gaijin* was hired to do a specific job or for specific expertise. Once the company felt it had acquired sufficient knowledge of its own in that area, or once a new Japanese manager arrived from Tokyo, the American became expendable. He was usually sacked.

A change in Japanese management was what Americans always feared the most. It introduced a new face into the picture and meant that all the gains achieved with the past boss were abruptly swept aside. It was like a new square in the game of Monopoly: Advance to Go, do not collect $200, and start over.

Granted, there is anxiety aplenty when a new boss enters the picture in an American company. But hopefully you'll have the chance to sit down, have a talk, exchange thoughts, and learn what is expected of you. Maybe landing that big account a few months before will be recognized. Not with a new Japanese boss. The odds are he speaks broken English and his comprehension is next to nothing. How do you get across to him any more than your name?

As too many top-notch professional Wall Streeters learned, their skills usually had little meaning and were rarely an asset at NSI. Time and again, those who relied upon their expertise to survive were sadly mistaken. They were normally the first to hit the streets.

The members of the clerical staff typically were not much bothered by the Japanese supervisors. They were left to the local submanager. These jobs were low-level, and the skills needed to handle them were not difficult to acquire. Those who filled these ranks were the high-school graduates, considered by the Japanese as loud and barely literate. This isn't to say that a clerical *gaijin* was immune to mistreatment. But the abuse usually didn't result from a poor job performance. It was triggered by the employee's salary level.

The starting salaries paid clerical *gaijin* were pretty much in line with the going rates on Wall Street. What a job applicant didn't know, however, was that the Japanese had predetermined the pay range for each *gaijin* job. A starting level was established, and a schedule was drawn up for nominal annual increases until a ceiling was reached. No matter how well someone performed his job, once he hit that salary ceiling, action was taken. If the company wished to keep the person (about as likely as its wanting to relive World War II), he would be promoted or given a new job, usually having nothing to do with his former duties. In the more likely case that the Japanese had no further use for the person, the "treatment" started. It could be brutal. The quality of the person's work would be denigrated and picked apart, even if it was the best work being done at the company. The Japanese supervisor would become rude and downright vicious. For the American, a day at work would amount to a mental Bataan Death March. Inevitably the person would be driven from the company, and typically he would leave with an intense hatred of the Japanese.

Another thing an American had to learn about the Japanese was that what a Japanese says isn't necessarily what he means. Japanese interact with each other in interpretations rather than in fact, and this is completely natural behavior in their culture. The spoken word is employed largely to make the other person feel good. A Japanese says what he thinks the other person wants to hear; as a result, if you're not clued in to this trait, you can pretty quickly think things are going a lot better than they are.

Part of the problem between the Japanese and the Americans, no doubt, was the short amount of time they had been working together. Between 1953 and 1969, when what was to become NSI in New York City was no more than a branch office of Nomura Securities, the staff was small and comprised sixteen Japanese nationals and a couple of locals. Gradually a few *gaijin* were hired. In the early days, only black Americans would work for the company, always at very low-level jobs. It appeared the sting of World War II was still smarting and white professional Americans wouldn't work for Nomura.

In 1969, when Nomura incorporated its American branch office as a New York company, NSI became interested in hiring some top-caliber Americans. During this period, Lou Riggio got involved in the corporate affairs of the company. Riggio found that there were no formal policies at NSI for hiring *gaijin;* it was done on an ad hoc basis. The local staff was growing, but not on a need-to-hire basis proportional to the expanding business. True, if a department really needed additional help, a *gaijin* would be hired. But then, not to be outdone, every other department needed more assistance, and a hiring frenzy would be on at NSI. Soon young American girls sitting around the office all day, chomping on wads of gum and reading fan magazines, became a common sight.

Naturally, the Japanese had their own personnel policies, but they did not apply to the non-Tokyo staff. To a certain extent, this probably was a blessing. As I saw it, the Japanese staff at Nomura strived for a "oneness." The company would strip all individual characteristics from the person and remold him into the Nomura man. Once the person had been stripped of his identity, he could then work better as a cog within his group. But, strangely enough, this oneness concept wasn't applied to the American operation. NSI was made up of independent groups operating apart from each other. The securities research department went its way, sales in a different direction, trading another, syndicate in still another. Each functioned on its own. The major objective was to make the section chief look good, sometimes an impossible task.

There was a good reason for this philosophy, should you be a Japanese national. If your section chief looked good, he might be promoted and the department would require a new leader. It could be you! If another section or division ran into trouble, all the better for you. There was nothing a Japanese liked to see happen more than for another department to hit the rocks. Those involved in a troubled area would have to share the blame for the poor performance, which was not a good sign on the narrowing road to the company's upper echelons.

There is an old Japanese expression, "The nail that sticks up gets hammered." In other words, don't be an individualist. There is safety within the group. All share in the rewards, and if trouble develops, many hands lighten the load of failure.

One day when I was struggling to understand the ways of the company, one of the senior Japanese executives explained his Propeller Theory to me. He held up his Nomura fiftieth-anniversary gold Cross pen to illustrate it. Pointing to the top of the pen, he said, "Up here is jeopardy." Then he pointed to the bottom end of the pen. "People here in jeopardy," he said.

Then he added, "At Nomura, strange things happen. Many time things get turned upside down." He flipped his pen around. "People at top," he continued, "now at bottom and people at bottom now at top. All still in jeopardy."

"The safest place," he said, "is in middle." He twirled his pen around. "Those in middle, no change, no problems, no jeopardy. Propeller spins around and around and people in center not touched by changes."

To survive at Nomura, in other words, don't be an overachiever and don't be an underachiever. Run with the pack and work to make your section chief look good.

Unfortunately, the Propeller Theory didn't apply to the

American brokers at NSI. The underachievers actually stood a better chance of survival than the overachievers. Several of the former lasted for years, and at senior management levels. They made the Tokyo staff look good, and that's what counted the most.

The message to the Nomura man was sell, sell, sell. Do anything to sell. For years, in fact, Nomura's ratio of salespeople to total employees was something like three to one, more than double the average of the U.S. brokerage industry. In my early days at NSI, though, I was more like a farmer than a salesman. I was planting the seeds, tilling the soil, and hoping a crop would grow by harvest time.

At the beginning of 1974 NSI finally assigned me thirty accounts, to which I was to sell Japanese equities. Curiously, none was among those I had previously had anything to do with. I never did find out where those names came from.

Of my thirty accounts, ten were Canadian banks and insurance companies. At the time, Canada had severe restrictions on investing in foreign securities markets. No more than 10 percent of a company's investments could be placed in overseas markets, and the United States was considered overseas. The Canadians were rather outspoken, and none had any interest in investing in Japan; they said so in no uncertain terms when I called them. They made it perfectly clear that they didn't want to encourage anybody to pester them with unwanted, repeated telephone calls pushing Japanese stocks.

The outlook for the remaining twenty clients wasn't any better. Two of them turned out to be branch offices of New York Stock Exchange members, Rotan Mosle in Texas and the now-defunct Edwards & Hanly in Red Bank, New Jersey. I asked them how their names happened to get on NSI's client list. In both instances, the answer was the same. Several years back, each had a customer who wanted a research report on Sony. They contacted NSI, which thereafter classified them as bona fide customers.

Several of the other customers were hedge funds (private investment partnerships) that had gone out of business. The balance of my accounts consisted of an assortment of small country banks that had had the same flickering level of interest in Japanese stocks as did the stockbrokers: A depositor had wanted some information on Sony.

In the end, just four institutions on the list indicated they might want to make some Japanese investments some day, though not in the foreseeable future.

After spending a fair amount of time culling this information, I filed my report with Saitoh, who in turn gave it to Kurokawa and Aono. When he reviewed it, Kuro became enraged and called me in.

"This is not what I want to hear," Kuro said. He told me I had better resubmit the results of the survey. Vinegar Andy and Aono gave grim smiles and nodded their agreement.

"How can I?" I asked Kuro. "Those comments were the direct quotations by the investment officers at the various institutions."

Cumbrously, Kuro's gaze swung to me. He just shook his head and refused to accept the report.

Some years later, Jules Spohn, who had also been a *gaijin* trader and salesman at NSI, told me about a similar experience. When NSI hired him, Spohn said, his salary was below the going rate for Wall Street companies, but Aono told him that what he gave up in income he would make up for in job security. Aono said that a position at NSI was the same as one in Japan: lifetime employment. This was pretty soothing music to Jules, for security mattered far more to him than money.

Spohn said the major complaint against him during his thirteen months at NSI was that he was not wringing enough business from his midwestern accounts. He said he was pressured by NSI management to get his clients drunk and fix them up with girls, the way selling was done in Japan. Then the orders would flow, at least according to the Japanese management.

This was not exactly Spohn's style. It was not his clients' style either. He repeatedly told his Japanese superiors as much, but they refused to believe him. So he made a survey of the customers and listed what they needed and wanted from NSI. Spohn said that what the Japanese failed to understand was how most American institutions allocate their commission business to the brokers. Once a year, their investment committees sit down to evaluate the services of each broker. The committee will decide how much commission the broker will get for the following year, if any. And that is what the broker gets. Sometimes it will be less, if business is slow, but never will it be more than the predetermined figure.

One day Spohn was called into a meeting with NSI's executives, including Aono. Spohn reported his findings. Rancorous scowls creased everyone's face. He was sternly told that that was not what they wanted to hear. Despite Aono's assurances of job security, Spohn found himself unemployed shortly thereafter.

My fate was a bit better. After my fruitless session with Kuro, it became clear that my days in institutional sales were coming to an end. Despite the gains I had achieved with the Midwest exchange, I was looked upon as having hopeless shortcomings as a salesman. Had I blithely told my bosses that everyone I called on was desperate to do business with us, I might have had a promising career in the department. In any event, Kuro did do me a favor. Rather than send me to the mailroom or make me the company cook, he shipped me out to the syndicate department, where I would have the chance to learn a new and useful trade on Wall Street.

9

Syndicate à la Nomura

THE SYNDICATE DEPARTMENT DIDN'T OCCUPY THE BEST location in the world. It was a cluster of a few desks on the twenty-fifth floor facing a narrow hallway that led to the ladies' room. As far as I could tell, the department was situated where it was entirely because of its low status, since the firm now had plenty of room. In February 1974 NSI had moved from its cramped quarters on the sixteenth floor, where it had about a third of the available space, to swallow up the entire twenty-fifth floor. Shaped like a reversed *L* with a long tail, the office was a bright, cheery expanse with ceiling-high windows, off-white walls, tan wall-to-wall carpeting, and heavy blond wooden furniture. Riggio had negotiated the move. Given a choice of either the twenty-fourth or twenty-fifth floor, Lou opted for the higher location, not for the slightly better view but because the Japanese are superstitious about the number four. They believe it is unlucky in the same way that Americans worry excessively about thirteen.

Despite its location, the syndicate department did have some specific and grandiose ambitions. It had been officially launched in 1972 with three clearly defined goals. First, it was to achieve market penetration by becoming part of as many underwritings as possible. Second, it was to get out in front and remain ahead of our Japanese competitors. Finally, if possible, it was to make some money. Judging from what I saw, though, profits were never much of a consideration in the day-to-day operations. Market penetration was what the Japanese were after.

The first time Japanese-American brokers got involved in U.S. underwritings had been as recently as 1970, courtesy of Merrill Lynch. Taking a step to internationalize the financial markets, the big American brokerage house extended an underwriting invitation to the U.S. affiliates of Japan's Big Four brokerage firms: Nomura, Daiwa, Nikko, and Yamaichi.

One or more investment bankers form an underwriting group for a short duration of time for the sole purpose of purchasing a new issue of stocks or bonds from the issuer for distribution to investors. The investment banker forming the underwriting group is known as the lead manager and the group is called a syndicate. The syndicate assumes the risk of buying the new issue and hopes to resell the securities for a profit. The securities are purchased from the issuer; a slight mark-up called the spread or commission is added; and the stocks or bonds are sold to investors at a fixed price. The lead manager will allocate securities to the syndicate members so they may fill their orders from clients. This allocation is called a retention. Sometimes the allocation may be more than an underwriter's commitment, but usually much less, because the manager will hold back a portion of the securities of the underwriting for selected large buyers. This portion is called "the pot." If underwriting is not sold, the manager requires the rest of the syndicate to buy those unsold securities. This portion is called "pot liability."

No one seems to recall the name of this particular bond offering, but I do know that the invitation landed on Lou Riggio's desk. After all, he was the only American professional then at NSI, and he was supposed to know about those things.

He didn't. It wasn't his fault, though. Lou had gotten his Wall Street start with Harris Upham, a firm whose policy forbade engaging in the underwriting business. Whenever he was in the dark about something, however, Lou had a standard backup policy: he called me. Since my Wall Street career began with Merrill Lynch, which was very much in the underwriting business, I did know something about the subject, or at least more than Lou and Nomura. My advice was to accept the invitation.

Later, Lou told me my advice was right on target. NSI accepted, saw its name in the newspaper advertisement, or "tombstone," got no bonds to sell, and several months later received an underwriting check. This was the Japanese's idea of a free lunch; all you had to do was say yes, and people tossed money at you. Why hadn't somebody thought of this earlier?

The day finally arrived, however, when NSI was given some actual bonds to sell. This made things a little sticky. First, NSI had no clients who would buy American securities (naturally, NSI wasn't about to admit that). But even if NSI had had customers, it would have been difficult to sell these particular bonds. The lead manager had been extremely aggressive and had clearly overpriced the underwriting. Therefore, it laid off part of its unsold inventory on the unsuspecting Japanese. It figured, let them take the loss. Those responsible at NSI were preparing to fall on their samurai swords.

As it turned out, I helped NSI dodge the bullet. Riggio asked me for suggestions, and I told him I knew a bond salesman at the firm of UBS-DB Corporation, a company jointly owned by the Union Bank of Switzerland and Germany's Deutsche Bank. I called my friend and learned that UBS-DB was indeed looking for additional bonds. They were willing to pay the dealer's discount or "reallowance." The reallowance is legalized commission splitting of the underwriting sales commission between broker-dealers. If a stock was offered to investors at $10 a share, the sales commission would usually be $0.50 per share and the reallowance set at $0.10 per share. The amount of the reallowance is established by the lead manager. Under these terms, any underwriter can sell shares to another broker at issue price ($10 a share) less the reallowance ($0.10 a share). In bonds, the process is the same. If a bond is priced to sell at $1,000 a bond, the sales commission might be $3.75 and the reallowance $1.25 a bond. An underwriter can sell his bonds to another at issue price less $1.25 a bond.

NSI called UBS-DS and sold its bonds. Some feeble life was breathed into the NSI corporate syndicate sales effort.

Not long afterward, the day of reckoning finally came at Nomura in another debt underwriting when NSI got what all syndicate managers dread, a "pot liability." A pot liability results when the lead manager of an underwriting has securities left over when the underwriting is terminated. The unsold stock or bonds are distributed to the other underwriting members. There's always a loss, because if it were a "hot issue," there would be no unsold securities in the first place.

So the bill for the free lunch was collected, plus interest. As Riggio put it, the loss had a sobering effect. It had rained in Paradise, and the Japanese didn't much like getting wet. In Japan, newly issued stocks and bonds rise in price, not fall.

When I joined the syndicate department, the division chief was Harunobu Aono, but he didn't sit near the rest of us, for that would have interfered with his true role at NSI, acting as a buffer between Kurokawa and the rest of the company. The day-to-day manager of the department was Yukihiro Terada. Terada had had a typical career with Nomura. He had joined the company upon graduation from Tokyo University in 1960 and, like all Nomura professionals, gone to work in retail sales. Terada told Riggio that he had made such a sorry mess of his clients' portfolios that he was transferred to the international department and then shipped out to the London School of Economics in 1968. Politically speaking, Terada claimed to be a socialist, a curious leaning for a man of international finance. He arrived in New York in August 1971 and was destined to spend the next seven years of his life in the United States, a particularly long stretch for any Nomura man.

"Mr. T," as he liked to be called, was short. Very short. He stood barely five feet tall and was stocky. He had a mouth full of teeth, black hair brushed straight back, and thick glasses. From a distance, he always looked extraordinarily busy. Whenever you passed him, he had his head bent down and was furiously pushing a pencil. Usually, all he was doing was cooking up ridiculous projects to drop on his long-suffering, browbeaten Chinese-American assistant, Alex Lau.

Barely in his twenties, Lau was about six feet tall and as thin as a reed. He kept to himself and did a good job; when not harassed, he did a very good job. His most famous act would not come until November 1, 1974. After putting up with NSI's nonsense for several years, he had had a bellyful of being a *gaijin* in a Japanese firm; so, as it was payday, he collected his check, gathered up his few possessions at five o'clock sharp, said not a word to anyone, and quietly walked out the door forever.

In trying to pep up NSI's sales force to sell U.S. syndicate items, Mr. T used a method slightly different from the approach employed by the American firms on Wall Street. Once a deal was priced, he sent Lau scampering down the aisle with an armful of prospectuses. He would hurl one on each desk and shriek at the top of his lungs, "Hot issue! Hot issue! Hot issue!"

There were several drawbacks to this strategy. The most obvious one was, there were no hot issues. NSI was never invited into any important deals, so the telephone never rang from any customers. Second, since NSI rarely got stocks or bonds to sell from an underwriting, it really didn't matter if the force was motivated or not. In any event, the salesmen had only one genuine interest: to sell Japanese stocks. That is what they were graded on, and in keeping with the Nomura policy, each had his daily sales quota to try to fill. Their attention was on the Tokyo Stock Exchange, not on some hysterical kid who, on orders of his boss, was running up and down the aisles.

Soon after my arrival in the syndicate department, but not because of anything I had done, business started to pick up. This first light at the end of the tunnel, however, turned out to be a four-alarm blaze.

On March 3, 1974, NSI stepped in front of a disaster called the Consolidated Edison Company of New York. The company had put up for a competitive bid $150 million worth of mortgage bonds. In those days, there were two ways to raise capital in the debt market. One was a competitive bid, and the other was a negotiated underwriting. Even though there were similarities, they were worlds apart in practice. Under various state laws, a public utility wanting to raise capital had to put its bonds up for competitive bidding. Anyone could make a bid, which would specify the terms and price of a proposed offering of securities. The various state agencies believed this method enabled a utility to get a better price for its bond issues at a lower cost. An industrial company, on the other hand, went the route of a negotiated underwriting, in which it would typically negotiate the terms and price of the underwriting with its traditional stockbroker or investment banker. An invitation to a negotiated underwriting was, and still is, difficult to come by. It is always up to the issuer and the lead manager (also called the book runner) to select which lucky Wall Street firms will participate in the underwriting.

There was usually a three-week lapse between the date an underwriting was filed with the SEC and when it was offered to the public. During this countdown, an underwriter had time to line up customers. Competitive bids, however, worked far differently, because nobody knew which competitive group would win until the bids were opened at the time of pricing. A competitive underwriting is an auction, and the best bid wins.

The managers of the various competitive groups typically invited their traditional bidding members, who had bid with them in the past, but the door was always open to any newcomer who wished to risk some bucks on a deal. In most of the competitive groups, the lead manager would change hands from year to year. There was an exception—Morgan Stanley & Company. It occupied such an exalted position that it was always the lead manager for any competitive deal it was involved with.

After a while, I was able to read Morgan Stanley's interest in winning a bid. If Morgan badly wanted to "buy" the issue, the meeting was run by Frederick Whittemore, Morgan's syndicate manager. He had the heart of a carnival barker and was a supersalesman. You knew then that Morgan was going to win the competitive bid and that the price and terms were going to be very aggressive, meaning the price would favor the issuer rather than the investors who bought the bonds. If Morgan sent its number two man, Thomas Saunders III, then it was a toss-up whether it was really all that serious. If they won, it would be a doable deal; you had a chance of selling your bonds. When Peter Cook, its number three man, showed his face at the meeting, forget it. You knew Morgan had no interest at all in winning, and it rarely did.

Two meetings led up to any competitive bid. The first came the afternoon before the actual bid. It was called a prepricing meeting, and at it the group would discuss bidding strategy. Strategy invariably centered on two items: yield and commissions. The meeting would be held on the premises of the lead manager's or book runner's office, and each member would send a representative to present the firm's views. A roll call would be made, and each person would be given the opportunity to voice a preference regarding yield and commissions. Needless to say, the larger firms underwriting several million dollars worth of bonds would be taken a lot more seriously than a small firm down for the minimum ante of $100,000.

The next meeting would be called an hour before the actual bid, thus at ten A.M. for an eleven o'clock bid. Nobody, of course, ever got there right at ten. A few would start to straggle in around 10:10 or 10:15, and the meeting room would be filled by 10:25. Dramatic entrances were very important, sort of like in pro wrestling. The front table was on a raised platform, and someone would be sitting there to keep attendance. If for some reason a member was not represented, it was assumed the firm wanted to be kept in the deal at whatever price was settled on. If one forgot to attend—and that did happen—it could be a very expensive mistake. About 10:35, the side doors would open, and the managers would file into the room. The book runner would take charge of the meeting with the announcement, "This is a competitive bid for . . ." and rattle off the name of whatever company was about to go on the block.

The lead manager would give the current condition of the bond market, the price levels at which similar bonds were selling, and a list of the institutional clients who were thought to have an interest in the issue. The manager would announce the bond's coupon, price, yield, and underwriting commission. Then each member would be called by the size of its underwriting commitment in alphabetical order. There were two responses: "Yes" or "Sorry, no." It was important to be polite. No one ever said, "No way, pals, this deal stinks."

The actual bid would then be given over an open telephone line to the syndicate desk to be relayed to the corporate finance officer of the issuer. Right at eleven, the issuer would open the sealed envelope, and the best bid won.

For those who remained in the winning account, the scramble would then be on to sell their bonds. Because there was no earlier preparation, they had only scant minutes to complete their sales. In a negotiated underwriting, everybody had the luxury of a few weeks to unload their bonds. But with a competitive bid, time was precious.

This was the situation faced by NSI on March 3 when the

Merrill Lynch account won the Consolidated Edison competitive bid. NSI was a member in good standing of the winning group. Consolidated Edison, in Wall Street lingo, was referred to as Con Ed. Many of the other utilities had colorful names too. Louisiana Power & Light was known as Lollypops; any of the three Chesapeake & Potomac Telephone Companies was called ChesPots; Commonwealth Edison was Seawees; the Wisconsin Telephones were Whisky Tels; Brooklyn Union Gas was BUGS; Northern Illinois Public Service was NIPS; and Niagara Mohawk was Slowhawks, because it was always difficult to find buyers for its bonds.

The Con Ed bonds were offered to investors at a price of 100¼ ($1,002.50 per $1,000 bond). NSI was given $1.6 million worth to sell to our clients. As we were critically short of customers, the best we could do was sell $30,000 of the bonds to several retail customers out of the Los Angeles office and another $20,000 out of our Honolulu office. The rest were totally unsalable—lemons of the highest order. There wasn't even a bid from any Wall Street brokers for them, so I knew we were in trouble. Deep trouble.

When the underwriting was terminated, the issue fell in price to 98 ($980, or a decline of more than $20 per bond). NSI was looking at an inventory loss of more than $30,000. Although I had just joined the department, I had packed away nearly twenty years of Wall Street experience. My unsolicited advice was to swallow the loss and get out fast. I knew that the longer you hold lemons, the more lemonade you wind up drinking.

Aono, however, not wanting to look the fool, said, "Not to worry." He flapped his stubby hand back and forth. "If worse comes to worst, NSI will keep bonds as investment. They yield nine percent and company will make money." This fit the classic definition of a "long-term investment": a trade that turned sour.

As it happened, the bond market proceeded to go into the tank. About a year and a half later—and after several prime-interest rate increases, a couple of discount rate increases, a dividend omission by Con Ed on its common stock, and actions by the bond rating services lowering the ratings on the bonds—NSI finally sold them. It took a loss of $468,875.

That wasn't quite all. Several years later, in the summer of 1977, Alan Standig of the Internal Revenue Service agreed with Aono's original contention. He said that the purchase of the remaining $1,550,000 of Con Ed bonds was indeed an investment, and he tried to disallow the trading-loss tax deduction NSI had taken on it. A trading loss could be written off against the company's revenues, but a loss on a long-term investment required a completely different tax treatment. NSI was staring at the disallowance of a deduction of $468,875.

In the end, the corporate treasurer told me, NSI was somehow able to wiggle off the hook. It seemed clear to me that Standig was right. But according to what I was told by NSI, the IRS never collected taxes due the American government.

Not long after the Con Ed debacle, we got mixed up in another doozy. The deal this time was two million shares of Dresser Industries common stock, offered to investors at $49.75 a share. The underwriting manager was the First Boston Corporation.

NSI underwrote 17,500 shares and, to our credit, found buyers. We managed to sell our original allocation and even went back to First Boston for some additional shares. The Los Angeles office did an excellent job. It sold thirty-five hundred shares to individual investors and another two thousand shares to Capital Guardian Management, a huge institutional buyer. The New York office did its part by finding a buyer for two thousand shares from the Boston-based mutual fund complex Fidelity Management; a broker-dealer, Newburger Loeb, grabbed another two thousand. So the underwriting seemed to be in good shape. Then a crack developed when Fidelity Management, which had indicated it was going to take a sizable chunk of the deal from other underwriters, decided not to buy and canceled all the orders it had placed with the underwriting group.

This was a perfectly legitimate thing for Fidelity to do. All investors have a right to return underwriting shares. The rules specify that they must be sent the final prospectus and be given sufficient time to read and understand the contents before consummating their purchase. If they don't like what they read, they can rescind their purchase order. In everyday practice, this rarely happens. In fact, if an individual investor ever cancels, the broker will be sure to cut that person off from all future new issues.

Institutions, however, do things a little differently. Most will place an order, subject to the final price. If one does cancel an order to buy new issues, then the broker suffers the loss, but the institution isn't blacklisted as an individual is. An institution gives out millions of dollars of business, so you don't snub it because of one bad order.

In the Dresser case, however, the Fidelity cancellation caused the underwriting to begin to come apart. As a result, NSI found itself with a grave inventory problem. During the several weeks between the time the stock underwriting was filed with the SEC and the time the offering was made, the price of the stock had moved sharply higher. This had greatly cooled off interest among investors, who don't like to buy stock when it's trading at a peak. Thus the initial demand among buyers evaporated pretty quickly, and the underwriting became "hung up" in syndicate. That means the deal failed to attract enough investors, and so there was stock lying around. In this case, a lot of stock.

All in all, NSI sales efforts were excellent under the circumstances. We were forced to inventory two thousand shares. Alex Lau and I had covered the waterfront. Everybody who might have been remotely interested in this stock offering had been contacted. A total of seventy-five hundred shares had been sold, and according to the Wall Street professionals, we had done a good job. But one person didn't think so: Ben Goodly. By now, we had gotten accustomed to calling him "Mr. Bumbles," and the last thing we ever wanted was to have him stick his nose in a deal.

Mr. Bumbles very much wanted to run NSI's syndicate department. And he figured that if he made a good showing in the Dresser deal, he might get his wish. Once the underwriting ran into resistance, First Boston was forced to support Dresser's price at $49.75. It had been supporting the price for four days, which is a long time to carry any stock underwriting in syndicate. It was evident to everybody that the deal was in bad shape.

It was at this point that Goodly presented himself to the NSI syndicate department. He had just come from a long luncheon. He announced that the Dresser issue was a "hot issue." He said the Scottish trusts were buyers. He started fishing around in his pockets and finally yanked out a crumpled piece of paper. It was a list of supposed buyers for Dresser. Presumably someone had played a practical joke on Goodly at lunch, and naturally he had taken the bait. Yet the Japanese nodded approvingly, taking Goodly completely seriously. Alex Lau and I sat there in total astonishment. Neither of us could believe anyone was this naive—or dumb.

Aono had no understanding of the American underwriting business. His primary duty was to be the company buffer between the staff and Kurokawa, and it was a full-time job. He accepted Goodly's tattered list of buyers with puzzlement painted across his round face and handed it to me.

"Fitz-san," he said, "Goodly-san kindly gave us this list of clients who are buyers of Dresser."

Goodly stood there with a smug expression on his face. Then he said, "Call First Boston and take down more stock. We can do a job on this." (Goodly, of course, had never sold a share of stock at NSI. That wasn't his job.)

What Aono and the rest of the Japanese staff didn't realize was that if this underwriting had been in good shape, First Boston wouldn't have had any stock to give anybody, nor would it have had to support Dresser's price for the previous four days. And they certainly wouldn't have given NSI the time of day.

Aono then asked, "Fitz-san, have you called these investors?" I knew what was coming.

I glanced at the list. We had actually done business with two of the six firms—Capital Guardian and Fidelity, the one that had walked away from the deal leaving everybody high and dry. Goodly should have at least known that. The other four had declined our offer. They wouldn't buy Dresser at gunpoint.

I told Aono, "Yes, I called all of them," and I recited the details of each conversation.

"Fitz," Goodly said, "you're not covering those accounts the way you should."

I could have belted him. The crack made me look bad in front of my Japanese superiors. It was the cheapest shot of a cheap-shot artist.

I couldn't hold myself in check. I exploded. "Ben," I said, "that is the most unprofessional thing anybody has said to me in my eighteen years on Wall Street. I can't think of anything worse than to make a fool of your firm by offering stock to institutions when it has been hung up in syndicate for four days. That's not even unprofessional. It's downright stupid."

The presidential advisor quickly backed down.

"Gee whiz," he said. "I was just trying to help."

"That's no help whatsoever," I replied. "If you really want to help, then take these." I handed him a fistful of order slips. "Make some calls and sell out our unsold inventory."

That was all Goodly had to hear. Over time, that tactic proved to be our lifesaver. We were to use it repeatedly when Goodly got on our backs, and it always promptly got rid of him. Hand him order slips—What? Me sell?—and he suddenly remembered a dental appointment. It was like telling your kid to take out the garbage.

Goodly, in fact, vanished from the syndicate area for nearly three weeks after being offered the Dresser order slips. After he beat a retreat, I turned to Aono and said I understood from the Street that the Dresser stock was likely to go down $2 a share once the syndicate terminated. Later that day, after the market had closed, First Boston announced that the underwriting group had disbanded. The next morning, there was a delayed opening for Dresser due to an imbalance of sell orders. The opening price was $47.75, down $2 a share.

Not long afterward, the Con Ed bond loss worsened and Aono fell into disfavor. Someone had to take the blame. And so Aono was replaced as syndicate chief by Terada.

The first objective of NSI's syndicate department was to secure invitations to American stock and bond underwritings. Once we got the invitations, the next step was to badger the book runner for securities so we could turn a commission in selling them.

When an industrial company intends to raise capital, it must file its intention with the Securities and Exchange Commission. The SEC passes judgment on whether the public offering can be made. Otherwise, who is to say that an offering to sell shares in the Brooklyn Bridge isn't a bona fide offering and worthy to be sold to widows and orphans?

Once a company submits its plans to the SEC, an announcement is released to the financial press and gets reported by the *Wall Street Journal* and the *New York Times*. Dow Jones, the owner of the *Journal,* also carries these filings on its wire service. We always kept an eagle eye on the wire to get a running start.

When I spied something of interest, I would call the lead manager identified in the Dow Jones announcement and put in NSI's request to be an underwriter. In a fair number of instances, we would get an invitation. Once I got into a groove, I consistently managed to get us into more underwritings than any other Japanese firm. Still, it was always difficult to judge just how successful we were. By American standards, the Japanese did not participate in as many as did American firms of equal size, but no one expected us to. Yet by 1979 the Japanese brokers as a group were in more than 60 percent of all American underwritings.

Starting in 1981, however, an increasingly disgruntled Wall Street began to retaliate against the Japanese by dropping them from U.S. underwritings. The major American underwriters felt they had done more than their share in supporting the Japanese brokers in this country. The Americans called on the Japanese brokers and asked them to support American entry into the Tokyo capital markets. The Japanese-American firms did nothing. They sat on their hands.

Actually, the Americans were storming the wrong gates. If they wanted equal treatment in the Japanese capital markets, they should have presented their case to the parent companies in Tokyo. In the Japanese corporate structure, people in a local branch office—such as New York City—took orders from Tokyo. Their job wasn't to promote a foreigner's interest in Japan. The American brokers didn't understand this procedure. Consequently, what the Americans did was create a two-tiered underwriting list. One side was American only. The other, much smaller, one was foreign. Today, when a Japanese brokerage firm asks for an underwriting position, it's told, "Talk to the London people." The foreign side has become the province of the American brokers' London offices. A typical foreign lineup will include selected Americans, the Europeans, and sometimes a Japanese firm. According to an article in the *Investment Dealers' Digest*, the American-Japanese brokers were in almost 60 percent of all U.S underwritings in 1980. By the mid-1980s, the Japanese presence had dropped to about 9 percent in these underwritings.

But back in 1974, despite NSI's number one ranking among the Japanese firms, Kurokawa wasn't happy. He came down on me because I didn't have advance knowledge of the underwriting filings with the SEC. "Fitz-san," he once told me, "you are not doing your job." This, of course, was "nonpublic" information he was talking about—inside information, the kind that put Ivan Boesky in jail. Kuro, however, didn't seem to realize that there was anything wrong with it.

I told Kuro that this information was considered inside information and that I didn't know anybody at Morgan Stanley, Salomon Brothers, or anywhere else who was willing to risk losing his job and going to jail to leak advance notice to NSI.

Kuro grudgingly conceded the point, but he was not happy. Actually, if anybody was likely to hear anything in advance, it would be the corporate finance officers. That was Kuro's area, not the syndicate department's. Wall Street corporate finance departments approach each other to comanage underwritings. Once the managers are in place, a filing is made with the SEC and then—and only then—does a firm's syndicate department get involved. The Wall Street syndicate departments are the marketing arms of the corporate finance departments.

One of the more useful parts of a syndicate person's day is lunchtime. Terada liked to make occasional use of lunch to develop and consolidate Nomura's ties to Wall Street's syndicate departments.

The Japanese businessmen were given a monthly expense account, the size of which depended upon one's position in the company. Terada was in what Riggio called the "lowerarchy" and had better ways to spend his allowance than on the Wall Street *gaijin*. Most notably, he had nightly entertainment expenses with his Japanese contacts. Besides, he had to take his expense voucher to his superior—Kurokawa— and nobody wanted to come into contact with Kuro if it could be avoided.

Because I was part of Terada's team, I would pick up all lunch tabs, put them on my American Express card, and give the voucher to Terada for approval. Mr. T would okay it and pass it on to the company paymaster. That way it didn't cut into Mr. T's expense quota, nor did he have to face Kuro.

One particular luncheon turned out to be a classic. Our guest was Donald Cooper, a syndicate associate at Goldman, Sachs. (He would later leave for better things and become very successful as a broker's broker.) We met Donald at Delmonico's, one of the better and more expensive restaurants in lower Manhattan. Initially, there was the usual getting-to-know-you small talk. Then it shifted to business. As a breather, Don turned to Terada and asked, "Are you married?"

"Yes," Mr. T replied.

"Any children?"

"Yes. Two."

"How old are they?" Don asked.

"Five," Mr. T shot back.

Don looked a little puzzled. "Five?"

"Yes, five."

"Uh, are they twins?" Don said.

"No," Mr. T snapped. "Boy is five."

I understood: In Japan, a boy's age is important to the father, a girl's isn't; she is the mother's responsibility. So I asked Terada, "How old is your daughter?"

Now Terada's face reflected confusion. He thought a moment and said slowly, "I think she is about two."

Don gave us a weird look, as if we had just announced that it was time for us to be getting back to the asylum. The momentum of the early gains of the luncheon had suffered a setback.

Near the end of the meal, Mr. T started fishing for a compliment. He asked Don, "Who do you think is the most professional of Japanese firms?"

Terada wasn't quite prepared for the response. Don said, "I don't think any of them are professional."

Terada never got over that zinger and harbored a deep seated resentment against Goldman, Sachs from then on.

Though lunch offered the best surprises, the afternoon was the most productive and profitable part of the syndicate day. This was when most of the underwritings—stocks and bonds—were priced and peddled to investors. This was the time to call your clients either to confirm earlier purchases or to try and sell the remainder of your securities. It was commission time.

Sometimes sales didn't develop as we had hoped. So we used other ways to get rid of our inventory.

I had steadily worked myself into Wall Street's syndicate sales network. During the 1970s, some of the smaller brokerage firms had salespeople who specialized in selling syndicate items. Each week all the underwriting firms mailed out a list of new issues in which they would be participating. This list was called the "new issue calendar," and the specialists who sold it were known as the people "selling the calendar." They did other commission business, but their major efforts were to market the securities their firms had underwritten. When one of us found a buyer, we would pass the word to our friends that, say, Chase Manhattan Bank was looking for bonds or stock in the new issue we were trying to sell. I would call Chase, sell the issue, and pass the word to a friend who would call Chase hoping to make a sale. This underground system worked out well and gave many of us a few extra commission tickets over the years.

If the underground network system failed to produce any buyers, I would turn to other broker-dealers to do reallowance business. That meant to sell the stock or bond and give up part of the selling commission. Most of the time this procedure worked. The few times it didn't, we took an inventory loss. That was an occupational hazard. Sometimes the book runner got carried away and overpriced an underwriting, and the buyers would disappear. When this happened, all the underwriters would lose money (as in the Consolidated Edison bond deals, where NSI took a loss of nearly a half million dollars).

Slowly, but surely, however, NSI began to do something rather unusual: It began to make lots of money. In 1975 everything began to click, and NSI experienced a loss on only 9 of 234 issues. This was probably the lowest ratio of any underwriter of that era.

According to NSI's files, that year our team established a

record profit that stood into the next decade. In the underwriting world at least, NSI had got its act together. For a while there, we were pleasantly purring along. Little did I realize that there was a freight train heading right for us just around the bend.

10

From Mitsui with a Kiss of Death

I N JUNE 1975 NSI ORGANIZED ITS SYNDICATE SALES DEPART-
ment, which seemed like a logical move, for it would be useful
in marketing NSI's underwritings. Actually, however, NSI established it for an altogether different reason. It wanted John
Johnson to have a chance to finally do some commission business so Kurokawa could justify giving him a raise.

Johnson was an amiable man who arrived at NSI in April
1974, when he was thirty-seven. He was quite intelligent but
had been dogged by persistent bad luck. He started off in the
research department at Merrill Lynch and then moved west to
become a portfolio manager. Like so many talented people of
the time, he fell victim to the brutal bear market that gripped
Wall Street in the early 1970s. Along the way he had gotten
married and fathered two children. When he returned to New
York in 1974 he was single again and unemployed. Friends set
him up with a round of job interviews, one of which resulted in
an offer from NSI.

Kurokawa himself hired Johnson and was thoroughly convinced the man was going to be a star salesman. In fact, when
the Japanese parent gave NSI permission to hire Johnson, the
approval came clattering over the daily news wire, to which
everyone had access. We all read that Johnson would be paid a
starting salary of $27,000 a year (by today's standards, that
would be about $70,000, a good salary back then).

Despite Johnson's background in securities analysis and

101

portfolio management, NSI stuck him in Saitoh's institutional sales department. Nomura sorely needed help in its research department, but all it really cared about was sales. As a result, John Johnson became the proverbial round peg hammered into the square hole.

Since all the major accounts were handled by the Japanese staff, Johnson was assigned the same bread crumbs that I had left on the floor when I was transferred to the syndicate department. Johnson gave it his best shot, and he did manage to scare up a small amount of business, but his overall results weren't any better than mine had been.

One day in early 1975, Riggio accompanied Kurokawa on a business trip to Boston. During the trip, Kuro mentioned that the semiannual pay reviews were coming up and management wished to give Johnson a hefty pay raise. Unfortunately, he hadn't generated any commission business to speak of. It always looks a bit silly, even to the Japanese, to reward someone for producing so little. Motivational authorities generally frown on it.

Clearly, Kuro had to save face for having hired Johnson; he needed to give him greater responsibilities and a bigger salary. So Kuro decided to start a syndicate sales department revolving around John Johnson. To fill it out, Riggio and I were also assigned to it, but Lou was to do double duty. He was to continue working in corporate finance while working in syndicate sales.

Since all the other Japanese brokerage firms routinely followed the Nomura lead in everything, they too set up syndicate sales departments. If we had opened a bowling alley, the others would have followed suit. When they learned of the syndicate sales group, they presumably figured Nomura had done some careful market analysis and organized several task forces before coming to this important decision. Little did they know it all sprang from Kuro having hired a man well qualified for Wall Street but stuck in the wrong job.

At first, the new department was rather loosely structured. John, Lou, and I were expected to cover all of NSI's accounts to sell, or try and sell, them the American underwritings, in addition to our normal duties. Actually, I was pleased about the new department, even if it originated for the wrong reason, because it afforded me the chance to get some credit too. Up until now, Kuro had given my sales commissions to the institutional sales department. He saw this as a necessary motivational tactic. "These guys work very hard but have no sales," he once told me. "They are becoming discouraged."

When I heard that, I was really rankled. I was producing a sizable chunk of the company's revenues, and yet the credit was being given to others as well. With the new department, at least, the *gaijins* would get the credit.

Despite the occasional new opportunities, however, life under Kuro could be pretty exasperating. Whether you were Japanese or *gaijin*, you were a ripe target for his bullying. As Riggio once said, "Kuro gets his jollies by pulling out butterfly wings. Since there aren't any butterflies in New York City, the next best thing is the NSI staff."

One day Kuro called me over to his desk. I didn't know what he wanted, but I knew from experience that meetings with him never turned into the time of your life. He tended to work on a rotation cycle with the NSI's staff, and my number came up about every six weeks. By now, I had gotten pretty adept at one-upping Kuro during these encounters, but that never stopped him from taking another shot. At best, if I had really snookered him, he might omit me from the next rotation, allowing twelve weeks to lapse before I faced another showdown.

"Do you call on Connecticut General?" Kuro asked when I sat down before him. Con Gen, as it was known, was a large insurance company which would later merge with CIGNA.

"Yes, Kuro-san," I replied.

"Who do you talk to?"

I smelled a rat, and to collect my thoughts, I asked Kuro if I could fetch my Con Gen notes.

"I think you should," Kuro said sternly.

Having gathered up my notes of recent telephone calls to Con Gen, I returned to the hot seat. Kuro again asked, "Who do you talk to?"

I rattled off the names, dates, and topics of all my contacts. I thought it was a pretty impressive rundown, but Kuro looked anything but pleased. He fished a card out of his pocket and read off a list of totally different names. When he had finished, he shot me a hostile look and said, "Why don't you talk to these people?"

"Kuro-san," I said, "they are stock traders. I have spoken only to the bond traders, because we have been underwriting only bonds, We haven't done any stock deals in months."

Kuro consulted his card and discovered the names of the bond traders I had spoken with near the bottom under "Bond Trading."

He had to save face now, so he switched on the charm. He mentioned that he had visited Con Gen just the other day, and though he hadn't met the bond traders, he had been introduced to the stock traders. "Very interesting, stock traders young girls, maybe twenty-one, twenty-two years old," he said. "All single."

At the time, stock traders working at institutions were basically order clerks executing the buy and sell orders for stocks and bonds of their employees. These were the low-paying jobs in the world of the trader, and because of discrimination against women on Wall Street, the entry-level positions were filled by them. That's why, in the 1970s, the order rooms of the giant institutions were mostly filled with women.

When I heard this, I couldn't resist. "Kuro-san," I said. "You were at Con Gen."

"Yes."

"You met all the stock traders?"

"Yes."

"You discovered they were all young girls and single?"

"Yes," Kuro said, a smile spreading across his face.

"Well, did you find out what stocks they were buying for Connecticut General?"

Kuro's face turned beet red, and his head snapped to the left away from me. This time he had no answer.

After about ninety seconds had passed, I asked Kuro if he wanted to discuss anything else with me.

"No," was the sharp retort.

I had just bought myself eighteen weeks of peace.

Even though Kuro was in charge of everything at NSI, he did not have direct command of a sales unit, and sales are very important to a Nomura man. By creating the syndicate sales department, he was able to plug up this void. Now he no longer had to rely upon me to distribute NSI's growing underwriting commitments. Meanwhile, NSI's syndicate department continued to chug along. A few changes had been made. Aono was transferred to another area in the wake of the Con Ed bond disaster. Alex Lau had quietly packed up his scant possessions and, as far as anyone knew, walked off the face of the earth. Terada was now in full command, or at least that's the way it seemed to the world. The truth was, he ran scared. He wasn't comfortable unless I was nearby to help him with the ways of the American market.

Even though the syndicate department was getting on the map, we still weren't much bigger than Rhode Island. But we were gargantuan compared to the rest of the firm. There continued to be precious little commission business in Japanese stocks and bonds, so the one area within the company doing business with local securities in the local market was the syndicate department. And NSI's internal reports showed that I sold nearly 65 percent of all the underwritings. The balance was spread out among the other syndicate salesmen, the institutional sales department, and the Los Angeles, San Francisco, and Honolulu offices. So I was the largest producer at NSI.

When Price Waterhouse came to NSI for the annual audit in the fall of 1975, all it could talk about were the huge profits generated from underwritings. Because of the nature of the job, auditors don't give out many compliments, nor are they easily impressed. Yet Price Waterhouse was stunned by the volume and profitability of NSI's syndicate department, so much so, in fact, that it felt compelled to say something. The phrase it used was "a gold mine."

Unfortunately, and to the best of my knowledge, this was the only time NSI's auditors would have such favorable comments for the syndicate department. Before long, they became scathingly critical.

In August 1975 a pivotal moment in the history of Nomura occurred. The development was totally lost on the outside world, but, boy, did we notice it inside the company! Terasawa was recalled to Tokyo on a normal rotation basis, where he assumed a top position in the international department, and one of his archrivals succeeded him as president of NSI. Our new leader in New York was a man named Keisuke Egashira. He was no stranger to the international arena, for he had formerly been president of Nomura Europe, which is now known as Nomura International, Ltd. But his managerial style was a radical departure for us.

Egashira's arrival launched a new era at NSI. Things were bad enough when Kurokawa acted like a schoolyard bully, but a true reign of terror came about with Egashira at the helm. Egashira's bite was deadly as a snake's—without warning, quick, and, for NSI's *gaijin*, fatal! In time, he would fire or try to fire nearly every professional *gaijin* hired by Terasawa. What's more, his actions never seemed motivated by business considerations but strictly by politics. Terry once told Riggio, "Enjoy yourself. You never know who the new manager will be." How true those words turned out to be.

Egashira acquired several nicknames within NSI. There was "KE" after his telex code letters, "Kay" to his Western friends, and "Peter Pan" behind his back. The latter was what the Japanese staff most often called him, and it was picked up by the dozen or so *gaijins* who now worked for NSI. He was given the name because of his soft, quiet voice and delicate mannerisms, which very much belied his true spirit.

Egashira was in his early forties and married, with two daughters who attended Catholic school in Tokyo. He was somewhat taller than most Japanese, about five-foot-seven. His hair was so wavy that many of us speculated that he had gotten a permanent. He very much kept to himself, favoring the opera, ballet, and artistic events rather than drinking and womanizing with his Nomura colleagues at New York's Japanese piano bars. The rest of the Japanese were very uneasy around Egashira, and who could blame them? He was cut out of entirely different cloth.

The Egashira era was to be characterized by blatant and bountiful securities violations. It shifted into high gear during the second month of his command, with the third underwriting of Mitsui & Co., Ltd., the giant Japanese import-export company. (The first issue occurred in the 1960s.)

The second Mitsui underwriting (under Terasawa), an offering of $20 million of convertible debentures the previous fall, had been an eventful occasion. The interest equalization tax that Congress passed in 1962 had recently expired, enabling Americans to invest in overseas securities without a stiff tax penalty. In floating its bond issue, Mitsui became the first Japanese company to offer securities in America since the mid-1960s. It wasn't really for the money; Mitsui had plenty of that. It was actually an advertising gimmick.

Nomura didn't care, for it was named comanager for the underwriting. The lead manager and book runner was Smith Barney, and Goldman, Sachs rounded out the team. The Mitsui underwriting would have succeeded in the Tokyo markets, but the offering ran into difficulties in the United States because Mitsui was not a known name among American institutional buyers, and the name was not on the approved purchase lists of the American institutions. Nonetheless, the NSI staff wound up giving a good account of itself. It sold nearly $7 million of the bonds, mostly in international markets, and was left with just $27,000 of inventory after the underwriting was terminated. By contrast, Smith Barney sold just $60,000 worth of bonds and Goldman, Sachs threatened to pull out of the deal altogether because it could sell only a paltry $20,000. Neither American underwriter had been able to drum up orders among its clients, because American institutions weren't buying foreign stocks and bonds then. NSI, on the other hand, fell back on its Japanese-based clientele.

According to Lou Riggio, a member of NSI's corporate finance department who attended all the meetings, Smith Barney insisted on the giveaway terms in order to bail itself out of what looked like a difficult underwriting to sell. Riggio said he was shocked at the way Smith Barney and Goldman, Sachs "blew it." The price of the bonds sold to a fat premium right away and showed a gain of 40 percent within a few months.

After the conclusion of the offering, Kuro singled out John Johnson for his magnificent contribution. Actually, although he supervised the marketing of the underwriting, Johnson was the only one in the sales department who didn't sell a single bond.

In September 1975 Mitsui returned to the American debt market, this time with a whopping $50 million of convertible debentures. The deal was priced and offered to the public on September 17. NSI's comanagers were the same as before: Smith Barney (the book runner) and Goldman, Sachs. The size was more than double the previous issue, since there was unexpected demand in the United States. NSI went ahead and took every order it could snare. This time the company ran into trouble. Major league trouble.

Unfortunately, Kurokawa had been misled by the first Mitsui underwriting, when the underwriters had had a glut of unsold bonds. Being guided by the past, Kuro freely confirmed orders to anyone who came to NSI with an indication of interest. Kuro naively assumed Smith Barney would give NSI all the bonds it could sell.

NSI underwrote $5,086,000 in bonds and received a generous $7,456,000 for resale to its clients. But NSI oversold its position by a shocking 40 percent, or $10,500,000 worth of bonds.

Nomura and Kurokawa, as well as Egashira, were in for a rude awakening. This time Smith Barney had no additional bonds. In the time that had elapsed since the first Mitsui deal, the Americans had learned what Japanese convertible bond underwritings were all about—and they liked what they saw. These were incredibly cheap deals that promised bountiful profits. As a result, the investment community had snapped up all the available bonds. Because NSI had followed the same pattern as the last time—sell, sell, sell—it was now looking down the barrels of a potentially mammoth loss.

As all of this was unfolding, I had no idea what was going on. The Japanese rarely tell their *gaijin* anything until it is too late to repair the damage. And this was one of those times. Yet I did have an uncomfortable feeling that NSI was in a serious fix. There was an obvious tipoff: Kurokawa was actually nice to me.

A few days before the issue was offered, NSI still had an oversold position of $3 million worth of bonds. About this time, I got a telephone call from an old friend named Albert Barbara, the syndicate manager at Muller & Company. The friendship between us dated back to the mid-1960s, when both of us were retail salesmen. Barbara was fronting for another broker when he called to ask how NSI stood with the Mitsuis.

Were we all sold out, or did we have some bonds to sell into the dealer market?

That was a leading question. Barbara was one of the very few people I trusted on Wall Street, so I confided to him, "We're short out of our minds, and we've got a big problem. It's along the lines of the one Custer had at the Little Big Horn."

"Well, would NSI be willing to take some bonds from another dealer?" Barbara asked.

Oh God, I thought. Does a bear like honey? This was one of those rare opportunities that present themselves maybe once in a lifetime. Neither of us, however, realized then just how far the consequences were to reach.

Barbara told me to sit tight and he would get back to me. He didn't give me the name of the dealer, but I knew Barbara was a person who could be trusted on both sides of the fence.

There was a bond house during that era that had a dealer-to-dealer desk. It was called Stern Lauer, and the department head was another friend of mine—William Morfeld. I called Morfeld at home that night and gave him an order to buy $1.5 million of Mitsui convertible bonds for NSI. It was only half of our short position, but there was no sense in totally exposing yourself. In the end, all Morfeld could round up was $300,000 worth. From all reports, this took a superhuman effort. The issue was tight and in good shape. There were just no available bonds floating around.

A deepening sense of doom settled in at 100 Wall Street's twenty-fifth floor. The seriousness of NSI's problem was sinking in. There was one saving grace: The bonds were not selling at a premium over the offering price. Had they been, the situation would have been totally hopeless. As things stood, we could still hope for a miracle.

The miracle came when Al Barbara called again.

"Is Nomura still looking for bonds?" he asked. I told him the guys here would sell their souls to the Devil for bonds—if they had souls to sell.

I asked him who the seller was, but he declined to say. He told me I would get a call.

I did. It was from Don Epifano of Ultrafin International Corporation, a now-defunct brokerage affiliate of an Italian bank. Somehow Epifano had bought a huge amount of the Mitsui bonds, thinking they would move to a premium over the issue price. He could then reoffer the bonds to his clients and make a profit. When it didn't happen, he became nervous. Al said Epifano always got nervous, but this time he was sitting on $1 million of the Mitsuis, so he had good reason to be edgy. Yes, he was more than happy to sell out his position.

I put Epifano on hold, walked over to a sweating Kurokawa, and asked, "Is NSI interested in buying $1 million of Mitsui?"

Kurokawa could scarcely believe what he heard. The storm clouds were starting to lift from this pending disaster. Yes, he said, and if Ultrafin could find some more we'd take them, too.

I picked up the phone, bought Epifano's bonds, and told him that NSI could use more, but I also mentioned that we had a bid out there with another firm. If Ultrafin was going to go against NSI's bid I would hear about it, and that would end all future business with me. Ultrafin and Nomura had done a large volume of syndicate business in the past, so Don had to take this threat seriously.

"What'll I do?" Epifano asked.

"You're a smart boy, figure it out," I replied.

There was a silence on the other end of the phone. I could almost hear the light bulb snap on. Epifano figured it out very quickly indeed. I had closed out the U.S. market to him, but Europe was wide open, and Ultrafin, with its Italian banking connection, could easily pull in some foreign business. Sure enough, he was to round up another $500,000 worth of bonds for us from his overseas sources.

Because NSI had sold $4,200,000 of the Mitsuis into the company's overseas system (thus creating the problem), my guess was that NSI was buying back its own bonds through Epifano, and at a higher price. NSI had actually given these bonds away by deducting the full selling commission, a violation of American securities laws. The way NSI disposed of the excess stocks and bonds it got in underwritings was to "dump" the securities by illegally eliminating the sales commission to the Nomura worldwide affiliates. This gave these affiliates an unfair advantage over the American underwriters, because they were able to reoffer these securities to clients at a discount from the higher offering price. If a U.S. underwriter gives such a discount, the firm is in direct violation of the National Association of Securities Dealers' Rules of Fair Practice. Such a violation could get an underwriting firm in hot water.

Yet NSI broke the rules and got away with it clean as a whistle. As a result, the company discovered a new way to "sell" its underwritings.

At the moment, Kurokawa didn't seem too bothered by legalities. He was much more concerned with NSI's potential loss on the Mitsui underwriting. With the final spurt of activity, however, NSI was able to dodge this cannon shell. After I broke the ice in buying bonds in the dealer's market, Kurokawa got into the act. He telephoned Nomura's London office and bought back $300,000 of the bonds that had been "sold" to them.

Looking back, it seems hard to believe all these transactions took place in a single day. It seemed much longer than just a few hours. It had been a nightmare that became a living reality. Once NSI's oversold position was covered, Kurokawa called me over to his desk to thank me personally. He even shook my hand, a rare event indeed.

At Nomura, things are never over, even if the fat lady sings. The second Mitsui underwriting came whipping back like an out-of-control boomerang.

On the afternoon of September 19, NSI received a message from Smith Barney: "Please be advised that we effected a stabilization transaction [in Mitsui common stock] on Thursday, September 18, 1975, at 9:00 A.M." The next paragraph instructed NSI to file their stabilization Form X-17A-1, attention, William P. Cummings. By "stabilization transaction" is meant a move to support Mitsui's price.

The twin red square flags with the smaller black square center were flying. I didn't read them as a hurricane warning. At first, I didn't think there was any problem. NSI had received $7,456,000 from the book runner, Smith Barney, and had purchased another $3,010,000 off the Street, for a total of $10,466,000. Nomura had sold $10,422,000 worth of bonds and had $44,000 in unsold bonds at the termination date.

I drew up the report accordingly and sent it over for Kuro's signature. When he received it, he called a meeting of NSI's executive committee, which was headed by Egashira. Terada was asked to sit in as an advisor. At the time, I was busy working on other syndicate matters and was unaware of the gathering. I did notice that no one was around, but that wasn't unusual at NSI. The first hint of trouble surfaced when Terada rounded the far corner of the office and headed quickly my way. His face offered no clue that anything was amiss.

"Fitz-san," Terada called. "Big trouble. Call Ultrafin. Have them change trade dates of Mitsui bond orders."

"What?" I said.

It doesn't take a Philadelphia lawyer to know that falsification is against the law. And here was the American affiliate of the world's largest brokerage firm stooping to this level.

"Call Ultrafin and have trade dates changed," Terada said. "NSI cannot report trades in SEC report." Terada must have been speaking on orders from NSI's executive committee. As best I could tell, I didn't think he liked doing this, but he was in the end a Nomura man.

I sat there and felt my heart sink to the bottom of my stomach. I looked at Terada and whispered, "Terada-san, that's security fraud. I won't do it."

After a pause I asked, "What's the problem?"

Terada said there were two problems. First and most important was that NSI didn't want Smith Barney to know what it had done. Second, there might be a legal problem. (No kidding!) Terada said the executive committee called Sullivan and Cromwell, its securities lawyers, about the legalities of overselling an underwriting position when you're a manager. The opinion was that it may be a violation of Rule 10b-6. This is a rule from the 1934 act that covers buying and selling of a security by a member of an underwriting before and after the security is in syndication. The question and the advice came long after the fact.

The executive committee nevertheless went off the deep end. It decided to conceal the fact by altering the dates and falsifying the report to the SEC. Thus Nomura shied away from a "maybe" position concerning securities violations and jumped with both feet into a clear-cut fraud.

I was the key man in this scheme, and my cooperation was needed and demanded. But I flatly refused to be an accomplice to illegal activities. Terada slunk back to the executive commit-tee meeting with the bad news. At that moment, I had an unshakable feeling my days at NSI were numbered.

As it happened, Riggio witnessed what had occurred and had a good piece of advice. "Tip 'em off, Fitz, before Ultrafin gets dragged in," he told me.

I phoned Al Barbara and told him what was going on. I suggested he call Don Epifano, because it was only a matter of time before Don would be hearing from somebody asking him to change the trade dates, and I wanted to be in the position to say I had not spoken to Ultrafin about this matter.

Sure enough, about thirty minutes later, Terada scooted around the far corner of the office once more, but this time he headed to his desk. He had a telephone call to make. He asked me for Ultrafin's number.

"NSI has a problem," he explained to Epifano. "Will you please be so kind as to change trade dates for $1,500,000 Mitsui bonds we bought from you?"

Terada got the same answer from Epifano that he had gotten from me. I knew that because he repeated it into the telephone: "No, you cannot change trade dates—violation?"

There wasn't much more Terada could do, except to beat a hasty retreat to the executive committee meeting and inform the others of Ultrafin's refusal to go along with the charade. Nomura was quickly learning that it was more difficult to do business in the United States than in Japan. The preponder-ance of American brokers obey the law.

After another hour, the executive committee meeting reached a decision and broke up. Terada was resigned to his fate. He was not in a position to spurn orders from Kuro.

He later confided to me the outcome: NSI would falsify the SEC report and destroy the files to cover up the problem. The company would take the chance that no one would ever com-pare the report against Ultrafin's records.

I sat there dumbfounded and watched as Kurokawa person-ally supervised the shredding of the incriminating papers from the Mitsui deal. Then Kuro got on the phone, called Nomura London, and ordered the people there to destroy all files relat-ing to the trades. No stone was left unturned—or so they thought.

One piece of paper, however, had been overlooked. It was the wire from Nomura London to Kuro confirming their sale to NSI of $300,000 of bonds and requesting delivery instructions. Terada picked it up, tore it in half, dropped it in my wastepaper basket, dusted off his hands, and told me he was going to the bathroom.

Naturally, the original stabilization report I had submitted never got out the door. Instead, a new one was drawn up showing on the bought side of the ledger Smith Barney's allocation of $7,456,000 of bonds and one additional purchase of $20,000 (incidentally, by Ben Goodly). The sold side showed $5,860,000 of bonds sold at the retail price of 100 ($1,000 per bond) and $1,500,000 less the selling commission of $15 per bond—even though that may have been illegal. This brought the total to $7,360,000, and Nomura reported a position of $116,000 of unsold bonds. That SEC Form X-17A-1 was dated September 24, 1975, and signed "M. Kurokawa, senior vice president."

There was no record whatsoever of the London trade in the report, nor of any other trades—namely, the $300,000 bought by Terada, the $250,000 acquired by NSI's trading desk, and the $2,140,000 I bought. The falsified report was then mailed to Smith Barney. Under SEC rules, the manager of an underwriting must maintain its files permanently. Therefore, Smith Barney presumably has these records buried somewhere in a musty filing box.

In the coming years, it would no longer be necessary for Kurokawa to soil his hands in this distasteful manner. Even though internal documents I saw showed that NSI would continue to dump underwritings by disposing of them to the Nomura overseas affiliates through illegal price cuts and falsification of reports to the SEC, Kuro found someone who would gladly stand in for him. He was none other than "Mr. Wall Street," Ben Goodly. His wish to take over the syndicate department was about to be granted.

Since Goodly's arrival at NSI, he had conducted a relentless campaign to run the department. He continually wrote all manner of memos about his grandiose plans, but more often than not he would forget to pick up the originals from the

Xerox machine. My friends in the mailroom were kind enough to make copies and pass them along. They could be pretty funny.

Like me, the middle management Japanese didn't take Goodly at all seriously. They regarded him as *moroku*, a Japanese word meaning "slightly dotty," and they tolerated him in good humor, like a favorite uncle who had never been the same since a concrete block fell on his head. After all, Goodly was no threat to them. But Goodly did have the ear of senior management, and they had no idea how underwritings were handled in the United States. So they took Goodly very seriously indeed. As a result, Goodly continually promoted a U.S. syndicate section headed by himself, assisted by some person I had never heard of. Yet his name was always in Goodly's plans. My guess is he was one of Goodly's down-on-his-luck buddies whom he was trying to promote onto NSI's payroll. The only time my name appeared on Goodly's proposed personnel charts, Riggio and I were lumped together at the bottom as salesmen.

Since Goodly's memos were usually back-stabbing assaults upon our department, every time I read one I was boiling mad and wanted to confront him face to face. The cooler head of Terada prevailed. He always lectured me, "Everybody think you stole memos. Nobody believe Goodly-san that stupid to leave memos on Xerox machine. You will be in big trouble."

"But he did!" I insisted. "He is that stupid."

One abandoned memo was dated March 22, 1975. It was four pages long, entitled "Why A Syndicate Department." It was subdivided into several parts: "Rationale"; "Difficulties"; "Basic Personnel and Equipment"; "Caution"; and "What Can Be Expected." It assumed NSI did not have a syndicate department. I guess the syndicate department we did have was a mirage.

The conclusion was that a firm of NSI's size and capital base could hope for long-term annual syndicate revenues of $308,250. At this very time, Terada's department was on its way to producing four times that goal. In other words, Goodly's long-term target would reduce NSI's syndicate income by three-fourths!

Sure enough, the syndicate department's revenues under

Goodly shrank nearly 75 percent by 1978 to approach his projected long-term target. For his accomplishments, Goodly was elevated to senior vice president.

11

Off to Siberia

IN THE LATE SUMMER OF 1975, NSI's MANAGEMENT SAT down to compute the next year's sales quotas. All in all, I had had a pretty impressive year, and I had been marked down to duplicate my performance. But that, of course, was before Mitsui came along and made a spectacular ruin of a lot of people's lives, mine included. For my refusal to play along and falsify documents in the Mitsui mess, I was handed some new marching orders as my punishment. Goodly finally won his long campaign to become NSI's syndicate manager. He was transferred from the president's office to a real job. With the arrival of Goodly, I was summarily ousted from the syndicate department and shipped off to Nomura's version of Siberia: the back office.

I was plenty mad. I had been working to build a reputation in NSI's syndicate department good enough to use as an escape to the real world of Wall Street, and I longed to bid a fond farewell to NSI's Twilight Zone. But then again, things could have been a lot worse. At least I clung to a job. And I had enough company for my misery. As it turned out, everyone in syndicate but our secretary got the boot. There was no beating around the bush. About three weeks after the Mitsui underwriting drew to its murky end, Terada emerged from Egashira's quarters looking alarmed, stormed around the corner of the office, and declared, "Everybody is out of syndicate."

I peered at him and said, "What?" I couldn't believe it.

"Everybody is out of syndicate," Terada repeated.

And so we were.

I found some consolation in the fact that Terada took a drubbing along with the rest of us. Because he was Japanese and on assignment from the parent, NSI's top brass couldn't get quite as heavy-handed with him. As his sentence, therefore, he was placed in charge of a newly formed American economic research department. He wasn't ecstatic about the news, for Terada had little, if any, respect for research. Before he got involved in underwriting, his job had been to translate and explain the hordes of research reports to Tokyo. Since most of the American analysts didn't really know what they were trying to say to begin with, and were less than adept at saying it, the mission became all the more miserable for Terada. The quality of the research was awful, and the results were even worse. Consequently, the last thing Terada wanted was to be known as a research analyst. About the only way he could galvanize himself to have enough interest to report to work was by playing a little game of make-believe. He simply decided that he wasn't doing research at all, but rather was furnishing "information." He even named his new department "information services," a designation it carries to this day.

With the dissolution of Terada's group, the syndicate sales department was adopted as a formal entity within the company. It was no longer a part-time job for Johnson, Riggio, and me. Under Goodly, Johnson was appointed the section chief, Lou Riggio was relegated to full-time sales, and John Ruff was added to the team.

Ruff was a bear of a man, well over six feet tall and weighing about 275. He was as easygoing as he was big, a pleasant guy to have around. He spoke fluent Japanese and had worked for Nomura in Tokyo for a year before returning to the United States in July 1975. When Ruff joined NSI, he was stuck in the institutional sales department and then switched to syndicate sales. Unfortunately, Ruff came onto the Wall Street scene about ten years too early. Had he arrived in the mid-1980s, his ability to speak fluent Japanese, his knowledge of Japanese securities, and his experience working in Tokyo would have fetched him a solid six-figure salary. In 1975, no American firm was even mildly interested.

Johnson's promotion came as no surprise. He had halfheartedly thrown his support behind Goodly's endless scheming to take over the syndicate department. After all, Johnson had signed on in sales and had not been as successful as he or anyone else had hoped. He too was looking for a way to expand his usefulness at NSI. Goodly seemed to hold out a degree of hope, and Johnson took the bait with gusto.

But Goodly was already planning to get rid of Johnson. He didn't particularly care for him; besides, he wanted to get rid of all the salaried salesmen to cut costs. His strategy was simple and diabolical. It was to hire "commission salesmen" for the syndicate department. Johnson didn't quite grasp that these commission salesmen were to replace him and the original staff. Particularly because of his support from Kuro, Johnson thought his position within NSI was secure. Like all the other *gaijin*, Johnson had been led to believe he had a lifetime position. But a lifetime for a *gaijin* at NSI always seemed remarkably short.

In March 1976 NSI added two more Americans to the staff. They were both commission salesmen for the syndicate sales department. In October another pair joined the company, and Goodly's trap was sprung on the original trio. Riggio, the biggest producer, would ultimately find himself rescued, but Johnson and Ruff were sent packing, without warning or notice. Ruff took it particularly badly. Sadly, he died of a heart attack less than a year after his dismissal, leaving a widow and a baby.

The syndicate department became nothing less than an execution chamber for *gaijin*. In the initial sixteen-year history of NSI's syndicate department, a total of seventeen non-Japanese professionals have worked there. Eight were fired, three were driven out, two resigned, one was transferred to another department, one was forced into retirement, and two remain. The few Japanese who have worked there are all still gainfully employed in the Nomura companies.

Normally, when a person is transferred to a different job at Nomura, the change becomes effective immediately. The person drops all activities and moves as fast as his legs will take him. My case was a little different. I was told to remain in the syndicate department for another two weeks to facilitate the transition.

After nearly two years of manipulations, Goodly had been given what he so badly wanted. But as Riggio put it, "Mr. Wall Street had no idea what to do."

Sure enough, the first bond underwriting Goodly handled turned out to be a nasty problem for NSI. The not inconsiderable inventory simply couldn't be unloaded. Here was his chance to put up or shut up. He didn't do either. He wasn't able to find a single buyer for the bonds and was ultimately forced to dump them for a loss.

Nomura's senior management knew Goodly needed all the help he could get, so they picked the brightest member of the junior Tokyo staff to carry him. His name was Haruo Miyako. Miyako, twenty-seven years old and an operations specialist, was appointed assistant syndicate manager. He was quite a bit smarter than most of the Tokyo staff, and this gave him a feeling of superiority. All Nomura men are arrogant. Miyako, nonetheless, stood a notch above the rest.

Shortly after the transfers were announced, he approached me and said, "As you know, I am replacing you in syndicate department. Could you give me one hour of your time to teach me everything you know?"

For a few moments, I was too affronted to do anything more than bite my tongue. Then I said, "Certainly, Miyako-san, if you can learn in one hour what it has taken me twenty years to learn, you've got your hour, pal!"

He got the message. He never approached me again.

It turned out that hotshot Miyako was not nearly as talented as he was supposed to be. He was prone to mistakes. Like most Nomura men, he tried his best to bluff his way through things he didn't understand and blamed the Americans in the back office for his blunders. This came to my attention when the American clerical staff repeatedly approached me for help, and with a long list of complaints about Miyako. Bad as he was, though, he was still better in my view than Goodly.

But Miyako was not licensed to do investment banking business in the United States. He eventually got his approval on November 19, 1976; for a year, he had been working without a license. If Goodly knew, he didn't seem to care.

Lou Riggio wasn't quite as lucky as I was. When he got booted out of the corporate finance department, he was told it would be only a matter of months until he was fired.

Egashira in the United States and Terasawa in Japan were rivals on the narrowing path to the top of the corporate parent. Both were managing directors of Nomura and wanted to become executive managing directors, the next rung up. It was only natural that Egashira would try to discredit Terry in order to further his own ambitions. But it had to be done very carefully.

It was rare for Nomura men to attack each other directly. Somebody else was usually used as the target. Because the intended person had not been confronted directly, there was nothing he could do. The person being attacked knew the assault was not for him, so he didn't care. Lou had been Terasawa's handpicked man, so Egashira went after Lou rather than Terry. It was political and had nothing to do with business.

The person calling the shots for Egashira was Kurokawa, and Kuro was extremely uncomfortable with Riggio around. He too had his knife out for Terry, but that didn't surface until years later. Kurokawa had been in charge of corporate finance for the Americas (North, South, and Central), and Riggio knew more about these areas than Kurokawa. Kuro's earlier attempt to claim Riggio's South American territory had failed, so Peter Pan had found an ally in Kuro. They started setting up Riggio to be fired.

Egashira gave Riggio two choices. He could work full-time as a syndicate salesman under Johnson, in which case he would be allowed to keep his vice president's title but would get no pay increase. If he failed to produce sufficient commission business within six months, he would be dismissed. The other choice was to remain part-time in corporate finance, where he would have three months to find another job. If he didn't find employment, he would be fired.

Peter Pan would have liked to can Riggio on the spot. But he had been the NSI president less than three months, and Riggio was too well thought of in Tokyo to be gotten rid of just like that. It was essential that Peter Pan buy a little time to build a case against him.

Riggio surprised Peter Pan by selecting syndicate sales over finance. What it boiled down to was that Riggio felt he was in a no-win situation, but he thought he had at least an outside chance of survival in sales. In corporate finance, forget it.

I was sickened by what was happening to Riggio. Fortunately, I was able to be of some help. During the time I was in syndicate, I had built up a comprehensive file of prospective customers. I had never had the time to develop them into true clients because of Mr. T's continual make-work projects. The file was a secret gold mine waiting to be tapped. With Terada's help, these records were secretly passed to Riggio. They proved to be the springboard for a miraculous comeback.

Riggio had learned to play the game the Nomura way, which was to make noise, and a lot of it. So he dug into my files and soon began grinding out $3,000, and then $5,000, a week in syndicate commissions. This was nearly as much as Goodly's long-term target for the entire department.

Several months had passed, with Riggio continuing his hot hand, when Egashira called me into his office. To my disbelief, Peter Pan told me that Riggio just wasn't working out in syndicate sales. Obviously, I knew this was not true. The department's daily and monthly reports were being passed to me, so I was well acquainted with Riggio's rousing success. Peter Pan said he was going to fire him.

Egashira had given Riggio six months to produce, and produce he did. Now, after just four months, the NSI president was going back on his word. I told him he was making a big mistake. Riggio had plenty to offer, I said, and he was being underutilized. In his whispery voice, Egashira said, "You are the only one at the company who thinks so."

I stared directly at Egashira and said, "Then I stand alone."

Peter Pan showed virtually no reaction. There was a slight flicker in his eye, and then he looked away.

Finally he asked me, "What would you suggest I do with him?"

My answer was that he ought to return Riggio to corporate finance.

"No," Peter Pan said.

My next suggestion was he have him do research in American stocks.

"He doesn't know anything about research," Egashira replied.

I told Egashira that in the early days of NSI, Riggio had made a daily report to Tokyo about what was happening in the American markets. Peter Pan had been unaware of that, but the news didn't cause him to change his mind. Then I thought I came up with the perfect solution.

I pointed out the good relationship that existed between Nomura and Merrill Lynch. Egashira could approach Merrill Lynch about Riggio; they must certainly have many places in their mammoth organization for someone with Riggio's skills. Egashira at least acted on this suggestion. It appealed to him because when a senior person is fired at Nomura, a certain face-saving drill is followed. The dismissed person is typically set up with another job at a smaller company under Nomura's control or a company friendly to Nomura. No explanations are necessary, for everyone understands the situation. He went ahead and contacted Merrill but, as usual, completely failed to make himself understood. Since he thought of Merrill Lynch as a friendly company, he expected it to react according to Japanese business practices. Naturally, it didn't.

Later on, Riggio told me he had several rather peculiar meetings with Merrill Lynch. He didn't know what they were all about, and the Merrill people were equally perplexed. Nothing, as a result, ever came of them. At this point, things were looking pretty gloomy for Riggio. At the last minute, though, when Riggio had one foot out the door, Terada rode to the rescue. He carved out a spot for Riggio in his new information services department, and Peter Pan grudgingly let him stay.

I subsequently found out that when Egashira had ordered the upheaval in the syndicate department, Terada had tried to come to the aid of both Riggio and me. He advised Egashira that such drastic changes would have a decidedly disorienting impact on the foreign staff and would foment a serious morale problem among the troops. Egashira's cavalier response was to become the company's unwritten corporate personnel policy. With an airy wave of his hand, he said, "*Gaijin* come. *Gaijin* go. *Gaijin* unimportant."

Of course, when Riggio was needed some years later, Nomura made no apologies in seeking him out. Even though the distance between Tokyo and São Paulo is over ten thousand miles, the long arm of Nomura reached out, far and deep, in 1983 to tap him on the shoulder. It needed help in South America, and Lou Riggio was by then with the U.S. Commerce Department as a commercial consul. In early 1982 Riggio had resigned from NSI to accept a limited appointment with the American government and had been dispatched to Brazil.

Nomura's messenger was Akira Inagaki of the Nomura Securities Brazilian office. In the early 1970s Inagaki had been one of the Tokyo people working in New York, so Riggio knew him from the old days. Riggio agreed to see Inagaki "for old times' sake" when he called for an appointment in March 1983. Riggio said he had no idea what Inagaki wanted nor, for that matter, what Nomura was up to in Brazil. Riggio added he was curious about the call, but not really surprised when he learned the reason for Inagaki's visit.

Inagaki's mission was to ask Riggio's help in identifying the potential investors in Brazil for a new mutual fund Nomura was cosponsoring: Sci/Tech Holdings, Inc.

Sci/Tech was offered in April 1983, and the $750 million offering was a then-record amount. The fund was an open-ended investment company seeking long-term capital appreciation through worldwide investments in companies deriving most of their sales from products and services in the science and technology industries; hence the name Sci/Tech.

The underwriting was a joint venture among Merrill Lynch, Lombard Odier International, and Nomura Securities in which each partner would distribute shares in its own part of the world. Merrill Lynch was to handle the United States, Lombard Odier would cover Europe, and Nomura's territory was the Asia/Pacific basin. Based upon the meeting with Inagaki, Riggio concluded Nomura wasn't honoring its end of the agreement.

Lou said his understanding was that in Brazil, Nomura Securities was only a representative office and not licensed to sell securities there. When he called this to Inagaki's attention, Riggio said the Nomura man's response was "You know how it is . . . ." Lou well understood. "It" was to sell, sell, sell, at any cost and with total disregard for any local customs or securities rules and regulations.

To the best of Riggio's knowledge, as he later told me, the Sci/Tech underwriting was not authorized by the Brazilian government to be sold in Brazil, no Nomura representative was licensed to sell securities in the country, and by agreement, Nomura was to distribute the Sci/Tech offering only in the Orient. Yet here it was, gearing up to do a hard sell in bankrupt South America.

Riggio pointed out it was just like the old days in the United States where the in-house company joke was, "the unregistered salemen sell the unregistered securities." Needless to say, Riggio was unable to help. Once free from the asylum, he wasn't about to visit on weekends.

12

Life with the Gum Chewers

My NEW AREA WAS LOOSELY DEFINED AS "ADMINISTRA-tion." Though I was now rubbing elbows with gum-chewing clerks fresh out of high school, at least I was no longer under the oppressive thumb of Kurokawa. Now I had two bosses, each a vast improvement over Kuro. Kiyoshi Kobayashi, NSI's senior vice president and treasurer, headed the operations department; Fusao Ishii, a vice president and assistant trea-surer, oversaw the day-to-day activities.

Kobayashi was in his mid-forties and had been educated at Keio University. He was one of the few people at Nomura who sought my advice and then actually followed it (as opposed to soliciting it and then, when I gave it, behaving as if I were from Neptune). Even though he was taciturn and mild-mannered, he had a habit that made him memorable to all who worked with him. He would sit at his desk, remove his shoes and socks, plant one bare heel after the other on the corner of his desk, and, with great absorption, clip his toenails. You could hear the loud snip of the clippers throughout the department.

As for Ishii, this story illustrates his character best. Shortly after I was shipped to the back office, Merrill Lynch ap-proached Ishii with a proposal and invited the entire cast of NSI's administrative officers over to its private dining room for lunch. I was included. What Merrill had in mind was to sell Nomura "repos," short-term debt instruments—such as CDs or notes—where the buyer can park idle cash to collect interest. The seller agrees to repurchase the securities from the buyer for a fixed price within a stated period. It can be as soon as the next day, with the buyer picking up just one day's interest. That may seem silly, but many of these transactions totaled millions of dollars, and the interest added up to a pretty tidy sum. Essentially, a repo is a fully secured loan structured like a sale and repurchase, with interest added into the cost of repurchasing the securities. Since NSI was cash rich, it was a logical prospect for Merrill Lynch.

There were about ten people gathered around the table that day to discuss the proposal. Ishii was the key decision-maker, because he was the money manager and was sitting on nearly $2 million in cash that was gathering dust in the Bank of Tokyo Trust Company. No doubt the money was earning interest in the repo market for the bank, not NSI.

Ishii immediately warmed to the idea and bought a $2 million repo on the spot. The Merrill Lynch man who was running the program had a tendency to get a mite overexcited. True to form, he jumped to his feet, sprinted to the nearest telephone in the dining room, and completed the transaction. He could have done it a couple of hours later, and it wouldn't have made any difference. Nevertheless, everybody was happy, and the luncheon settled down into routine small talk.

Everyone was quietly chatting when Ishii, clearly bothered by something, screwed up his thin face and asked a question that silenced the table. "Tenants' association," he announced. "What is tenants' association?"

Everybody sat back and stared at Ishii. I explained that it was a pressure group formed to force a landlord to provide services to an apartment building.

Ishii allowed the explanation to sink in. One could practically hear the wheels turning inside his head. Then he looked at me and said, "Next-door neighbor president of tenants' association. He tell me I am bad husband. Why he say that?"

Nobody knew what to answer. The Merrill Lynch man who had so dramatically placed the $2 million order was starting to look a touch uneasy.

Apparently to demonstrate how preposterous such a charge was, Ishii went on. "I get up in the morning. Eat breakfast. Drive to work with colleagues. Work hard all day. Leave office maybe seven-thirty. Go to dinner with colleagues. Then to piano bar. Talk with entertainment ladies. Drink. Get drunk.

Play mah-jongg. Go home eleven o'clock. Saturday get up early. Play golf with colleagues all day. Go to piano bar at night. Get drunk. Go home maybe eleven or twelve. Sleep all day Sunday. Give wife plenty of money. She take care of home and children. I don't interfere in house or with children."

Ishii then glanced around the luncheon table and asked again, "Why next-door neighbor say I am bad husband?"

I was the only one who had any further comment. I said, "Why don't you resign from the tenants' association?"

Ishii was famous as one of the champion check-grabbers in New York City. With blazing speed, he scooped up all the tabs for the NSI company parties. In those days, NSI threw at least one banquet a month for the professional staff. On top of these festivities were the usual celebrations for various milestones like the arrival of new people from Tokyo, the departure of old people for Tokyo, or anything else that could justify some free grub. As NSI added more and more *gaijins*, however, these celebrations became increasingly restricted to the Tokyo people.

One of the great ironies of NSI's decision to kick me out of the syndicate department for refusing to be party to a crime was that it then placed me in a position where I could witness virtually everything that went on in the company—the good, the bad, and the very ugly. But then, nothing else made much sense there, so why should this?

I was assigned multiple tasks in the back office, one of which was to serve as personnel manager of the company's *gaijin* staff. My responsibilities mainly consisted of hiring clerical personnel for the New York office. This was entirely foreign to me, and Ishii tried to be helpful and well-meaning when he gave me the names of several employment agencies and a few words of caution. Riggio had warned me many times, "Always expect the unexpected," but I was still jolted when Ishii leaned over and whispered into my ear, "Japanese don't like blacks. They are stupid. Don't hire any."

Now what do I do? I thought. I ran to Riggio for help. He told me I had no real choice. "You can't stop employment agencies from sending over blacks, but they won't be hired anyway. You'll be blamed by the Nomura management for introducing them into the company. You'll be asking for trouble." Riggio was opposed to this unwritten policy, but was giving me the facts of life at NSI.

In time, some of the employment agencies did send some blacks over to NSI to be interviewed. Most agencies were cognizant of the problem, so they were careful not to embarrass the candidate or me. As a result, I saw only a handful. Most of them were from the West Indies and spoke with pronounced Anglo-Caribbean accents. Since the Japanese staff had their ears tuned to American English, it actually could have presented a problem in communication. The other difficulty was the lack of a green card.

However, one particular lady I saw was extremely qualified as a secretary/administrative assistant. NSI had an opening, and she was perfect for it. Previously she had worked in Washington for a congressman. But she was black, and there was no way I could get her approved. So I had no recourse but to simply file away her application.

At a later date, NSI was to add "no Jews" to its no-blacks policy. NSI's trading department had hired a floor clerk from a New York Stock Exchange firm. Nomura actually thought it was getting a floor partner, a blunder that in this instance paid off. In time, he was to become a first-rate professional. Because of his efforts, the NSI American stock trading desk got off the ground and started expanding. About a year later, another *gaijin* trader was added, as well as an assistant. All three were Jewish. Soon after the new additions were firmly in place, a problem arose. It was the Jewish holiday of Rosh Hashanah and then, ten days later, Yom Kippur. NSI's trading department was incapacitated.

Even though Ishii had not been involved in hiring the Jewish traders or trading assistant, he had gotten a few complaints from his superiors. He passed the barbs along to me, adding, "Don't hire any more Jews. They take too many holidays."

Since it was much easier to smuggle Jews past NSI's management than blacks, I was pretty much able to ignore that order.

At the time I was appointed personnel manager, the NSI clerical staff was not of as high a caliber as it should have been. I soon discovered why. NSI routinely hired the first person interviewed for a job. A number of employment agencies discerned this habit and thus sent Nomura their most marginal applicants. Most were all but unemployable until they trotted over to NSI, where they were snapped up with great enthusiasm. After a while, some of these neophytes would acquire enough training and experience to qualify for better jobs elsewhere and would quit. Others were driven from the company. The women were usually the targets of the most abusive treatment. They would last be seen scampering out of the office in tears. The Tokyo people were somewhat more circumspect with the American men. After all, these guys might physically turn on them, and who wanted to get roughed up by some *gaijin* thug!

I quickly put a stop to the first-in, first-hired practice. I discovered there was a tremendous pool of talent in the job market at the time, most notably women who were recent collect graduates with degrees in education. Throughout their lives they had been led to believe there would always be a demand for schoolteachers. By 1976, however, the baby boom in the United States had crested, so enrollment in elementary and secondary schools was dwindling. There were no openings for teachers, and these young women were compelled to juggle their employment objectives and goals. Many were willing to work as secretaries or at any kind of job, just to have work. Meanwhile, they continued their search for professional entry level positions in other fields.

Knowing what I did about the attitudes of the Japanese toward American women, I felt bad offering them a job at NSI. But times were difficult, so maybe I was doing them a favor. Slowly but surely, I was able to upgrade the clerical staff.

Later, things took a sharp turn for the worse. NSI managed to negotiate employment fees to agencies down to 5 percent to save money. The standard fees were 10 percent on the first $10,000 in salary, plus 1 percent of every $1,000 over $10,000. The owner of one employment agency told me, "Who do you think I am going to send over to Nomura? If I can place somebody at the higher fee, I am going to do it. All NSI sees from me are people who get turned down all over town." Not surprisingly, the quality of local employees once again plunged and the turnover rate skyrocketed. People came and went so fast, hardly anybody got to even know their names or what they looked like.

In the summer of 1976 Nomura began setting up a subsidiary called Nomura Capital Management Company, the function of which was to run and manage an American mutual fund of Japanese stocks. It also created a new position of compliance officer, who would be responsible for making sure the firm obeyed all securities regulations. Because I was the personnel manager, I became involved in the recruitment process for the staff of Nomura Capital as well as the job of compliance officer. Two of the people hired were *gaijins*, and both were to play pivotal roles in the company over the next ten years. Both looked solid on paper, which is why I recommended them, but once they were hired their characters proved altogether different than I had figured.

One was John Frederick (Jack) Wallace, who joined the new Nomura Capital as secretary and director, and the other was Andrew Michael Basile, who became the compliance officer. They didn't have much in common, except they were both born in Brooklyn. Before long, they became known as the "Bobbsey Twins of NSI." Wallace had the ear of senior management, but that was it, and Basile was willing to do anything to further himself. They were a natural team.

Jack Wallace was in his late forties and resembled Jack Lemmon. He liked to wear a vest with a gold watch-chain passing through a buttonhole. It gave him the scholarly look of a laid-back intellectual. He wasn't. By the time he arrived at Nomura, Wallace had some eighteen years of mutual fund management experience under his belt. He also had a surprise for me on his U-4 form, the standard registration form that gets filed with the sundry regulatory agencies. One question on the form required all lawsuits to be listed. Most people neglect to think of their divorce and omit it. The authorities inevitably pick it up, to everyone's chagrin. Wallace, as it happened, didn't have a divorce to forget, but he did have a long list of other suits. There were so many, in fact, that they spilled over to an additional page. Most were shareholder suits that arose from his past management positions with other mutual fund companies, and though there were no findings of wrongdoing against him, it was a surprising number of lawsuits just the same.

When queried about the suits, Wallace didn't bat an eyelash. He actually seemed rather proud of their abundance. "You can tell a person's success on Wall Street by the number of lawsuits he has," he declared. I suppose he knew what he was talking about. He eventually became senior vice president and the first *gaijin* to sit on NSI's board of directors.

Personally, I used to think of him as Jack "I Don't Know Anything About That" Wallace. That was his standard, reflex response to just about any question put to him. On the other hand, no one could accuse him of misrepresentation. He probably didn't know anything. The other nickname he acquired was "the Governor," after former governor George Wallace.

I must say, his "I don't know anything about that" answer served him exceedingly well, for he earned promotion after promotion. According to Andy Basile, however, Wallace's automatic answer changed as he moved up the corporate ladder. Once inside the hierarchy of the company, he could no longer get away with pleading blissful ignorance. That proved to be no problem, for, like most senior executives, he found an even better response. And so he became known as Jack "Not My Area" Wallace.

In the beginning, Wallace must have been very insecure in his job. He tipped his hand at NSI's 1976 Christmas party, when I congratulated him on being named comanager of the operations department. For some reason, the NSI president had not yet informed Wallace. Jack registered his surprise with a double-take directly from the vaudeville stage. Then he blurted out, "Does that mean there's competition between us?"

I assured him there wasn't any, but I got the feeling that I had better watch myself around the president's new fair-haired boy.

Later, I got a taste of his mode of operation. In 1975 I was asked by Kobayashi to draw up a company employee handbook. The outline and original work had been done by the president's secretary, Yukiko Murata, the daughter of NSI's former chairman. She had done a perfectly fine job, but because she was a woman, Nomura management didn't take her work seriously. It was turned over to me for completion. I became the publisher, coauthor, and circulation manager. It was a first at NSI and served the company for years. Jack Wallace was the only person to question the contents.

The handbook had been out about a year and nine months when Wallace found fault with it. He insisted on immediate revisions and issued his complaints in writing. He claimed the book was "dated" and "inaccurate in parts." However, he failed to specify how it was dated or which parts were inaccurate. I was also told not to contact the NSI lawyers, prompting me to question how serious he was. Nevertheless, I made some revisions and turned them over to Jack, and nothing more was said. The original handbook remained in place for years.

I thought I made a good hire in Andy Basile. In trying to find a compliance officer, I quickly discovered there were more candidates than jobs, so there was a reasonable pool to choose from. Yet no matter how many people I interviewed, Basile still seemed to stand out from the rest. He appeared tough and hard-nosed, exactly what you would want for a compliance officer.

Basile was nearly thirty. He was only five-foot-five but wore extra leather in the heels of his shoes to give himself another inch. He walked from heel to tiptoe, so he bobbed up and down in a floating motion as he rambled around the office. His thick glasses gave him a pop-eyed look. He liked to think of himself as a "dead-end kid from Brooklyn." Andy had been an examiner with the National Association of Securities Dealers before becoming unemployed; I hired him off the breadline.

He was given the desk next to mine, and we got to be fairly friendly since we shared some of the same frustrations working for NSI. He entertained me with his endless stories about what a tough guy he was and how streetwise he had become.

Besides personnel, one of my other areas of responsibility in the back office was insurance. Actually, I filled more of a supporting role, for day-to-day operations were handled by a Japanese woman named Michiko Higa. She also kept all the confidential records under lock and key in a large, two-drawer metal filing cabinet that sat on wheels and rested beside her desk. If you wanted to look at them, you had to have a good explanation.

As an example of what sort of insurance matters I got involved in: One morning my phone rang, and Terada was on the other end. "Fitz-san, Fitz-san, confidential, confidential, don't tell anybody," he said.

I wasn't sure what was coming next. Since Terada was the company gossip, it could be anything.

"This morning I had car accident," Mr. T continued. "Hit from behind."

I decided to have a little fun with him, so I made the old joke, "Tell me something, Terada-san, how fast were you going when you backed into the other car?"

There was a long pause. Then, in his clipped, fast English, Mr. T said, "Howdidyouknowthat? Whotoldyou? Whotoldyou?"

Driving had been treacherous that morning because of the winter weather. On his way to work, Terada made a right-hand turn at an intersection, and his car hit a patch of ice and skidded. After the car came to a stop, he put it in reverse and slammed into the car coming up behind him. He was never to believe that I had taken a wild guess.

With some of the matters under my jurisdiction, it was usually better if I didn't get directly involved. One such thing occurred regularly during the NSI lunch hour, which usually lasted from noon until two. About 1:15 some of the local back office girls would drift back to their desks and be entertained by one or two of the American traders. The back office was separated from the rest of the office by a wall and door, but this didn't stop the gaijin traders from barging into the area to joke around with the girls. And the girls loved it. They were all very loud and disruptive.

In an American company, I would have kicked the traders out. But I couldn't do that at NSI. If I did, you could be sure I would have been the person who landed in trouble. Because the Japanese ran the company, no American had any say in management. In this case, the traders would have left our area, returned to their work post, and bitched about me to their

Japanese supervisor. And then I would have been in hot water, not because I would have ruffled the *gaijin* traders' feathers, but because the Japanese chief trader would have taken it as a personal attack on him.

At the time, Masayuki "Rocky" Iwai was in charge of NSI's trading department. Naturally, he would have thought the worst, that I was assailing him for something through his *gaijin* traders. He would have complained to NSI's president. The complaint would have crossed over to my supervisor, and he would have come down on me like a sledgehammer.

Knowing this, I turned to Ishii and asked, "Ishii-san, aren't some of the traders bothering our staff?"

Ishii looked up from his work. The racket was earsplitting. He nodded.

"Don't they have anything to do?" I said. "Why must they come into our area and disrupt our work? Doesn't their supervisor have better control over his department?"

That was all Ishii needed to hear. Actually, he had been searching for an opportunity to put a stop to this daily routine, but he couldn't think of the appropriate approach. He snatched up his phone and punched the extension of the traders' supervisor, Iwai. His Japanese was quick and short. He hung up, looked at me, and grinned.

About ten minutes later, the traders disappeared, never to return again. To this day, I don't know what happened on the other side of the door between the operations department and the trading department.

I do know that Iwai was a character in his own right and was building a small legend for himself in the trading department. He looked something like a statue of Buddha, but with a full head of black curly hair. He had convinced NSI's executive committee to give him a $3 million account to trade American stocks so he could learn all about the New York Stock Exchange. Since he had the reputation of being one of the more successful stock traders in Tokyo, nobody voiced any objections to giving him his head to run wild through the canyons of Wall Street and show the *gaijin* how it was done in Tokyo. It was to be a costly lesson.

Since the American marketplace is, or at least was, an open, fluid market usually devoid of manipulations and insider trading, a stock's price is based upon supply and demand. This makes the New York Stock Exchange a far different place than Tokyo's "managed" market. It is like shooting fish in a barrel for a Nomura trader to make money in Tokyo, because Nomura dominates that market. And Iwai sat in a position to see the ebb and flow of orders. He had no such edge in New York City.

At NSI you could always tell what the New York market was doing on any given day, or more specifically, how Iwai was doing. All you had to do was take a quick peek at the "Iwai Indicator." This was the position of the zipper on his pants. If Rocky was having a good day, he would be gloating as he strutted around the office. His hands would be thrust in his pockets, and his fly would be wide open. If he was having a bad day, he would still be walking around the office, because he wanted to get away from the trading department, and his hands would still be in his pockets. But most of the bounce would be gone from his step, and his zipper would be all the way up. The zipper half down signified a moderately success-ful day.

No one knew for sure what accounted for the reliability of this indicator—and it was very reliable. The best any of us could figure out was that if Iwai was on a roll, he didn't want to leave the trading desk. So he would rush to the men's room, take care of his business as expediently as possible, and sprint back without bothering to put himself back together.

Unfortunately for Rocky and NSI (and to the relief of the young secretaries), his zipper was up far more often than it was down. In fact, Iwai lost nearly $1.5 million of company money before he was "promoted" and sent back to Japan.

When Kobayashi and Ishii returned to Japan in January 1977, the operations and administration department was reorganized and carved up into five sections. Administration, general af-fairs, and office services were assigned for supervision to Ka-zuo Shimoda, Kobayashi's replacement. Back office operations and personnel were put under the stewardship of Jack Wallace. My areas were administration and general affairs, along with personnel. Thus I was to serve under two masters, neither of whom had the faintest idea how to administer his new assign-ments.

It got to be rather hairy at times. For example, NSI's insurance agent, the Waldron-Mahoney Agency, had served NSI for more than twenty years. For some reason never explained, Wallace got it into his head that I had brought the agency to NSI. Wallace made life difficult for both the agency and me with continual nitpicking demands. This finally reached a peak when I was called into the president's office and threatened by Egashira. Wallace was sitting in on the meeting. I was completely puzzled, but when Wallace mentioned "your buddy Ward Olney" (Mahoney's son-in-law) at one point, it quickly became clear what this was all about. I corrected Wallace and told him of the long-standing relationship between NSI and Waldron-Mahoney. That saved the relationship between the two firms and, fortunately for me, put a stop to the senseless demands over insurance matters.

Kazuo Shimoda was something else. In his late thirties, a graduate of Hiroshima University, he was very different than Kobayashi. In an organization where conceit is normal, Shimoda was a superstar. He was once quoted as saying "Only thing I cannot do is to have a baby." Two weeks after he had arrived in the United States, he was giving a local Japanese secretary advice on the dos and don'ts in New York City. She spoke perfect English, had lived in New York for ten years, and had taught in the New York City school system before coming to NSI.

Even though he claimed there was only one thing he couldn't do, there were two others that ought to have been on his list. He never learned to speak English, and he failed the registered principal's examination five times. A key NSI officer, a director and senior vice president, he was unlicensed during his entire stay in the States.

Apparently tests were hard for Shimoda. The New Jersey driver's test was another case in point. According to a story that made the rounds of the office, one day Shimoda and his lackey, Hiroshi Nagahiro, disappeared from the back office. "Sonny and Cher," as they were referred to, often vanished, as did most of the other Japanese officers, without mentioning to anyone where they were going or when they would return. (The most extreme version of this occurred the time when Aono took his vacation and failed to notify anyone. After several days, as his telephone messages piled up and senior management grew incensed at his absence, it finally came out what had happened. His secretary ended up getting the blame for not knowing he was on vacation.)

Some days later, the story circulated about how Shimoda had gone off to take his driver's test. It seems that when his name was called, he jumped up, jerked his fists up in front of him, and jogged out to his car. We envisioned it being like something out of a World War II newsreel, the kamikaze pilot trotting out to his plane to make his final flight. Shimoda reached the passenger's door, jerked it open, and gave the inspector a deep, polite bow as the man slipped in. Shimoda then trotted around to his side and jumped in behind the wheel.

According to office legend, Shimoda revved up the engine to a noise level that brought everything within earshot to a complete standstill. He then put the car into reverse, and it exploded backward out of the parking space. Shimoda gave the wheel a quick snap turn and threw the car into low gear. The smoking tires peeled rubber the length of the block. Nobody knew how fast the car was going when it reached the end of the street, but I was told Mario Andretti would have had trouble keeping up. Another sharp turn of the steering wheel sent the car through the intersection—sideways. The car then disappeared.

Nagahiro, who relished the opportunity to tell the story, watched from the parking lot in terror. Then he heard another squeal of tires to his right. He looked in that direction, filled with horror. Sure enough, here came Shimoda into the intersection, sideways of course. The car gathered another head of steam before Shimoda slammed on the brakes and skidded to a stop inches short of the restraining barrier. The tire marks were fifteen yards long.

Out strutted a proud Shimoda. He trotted around to the passenger side and flung open the door. Once more he bowed and declared, "See. I can drive."

The inspector was chalk white. Nagahiro claims he had wet his pants and was unable to get out of the car. He had to be helped out and sent home for the rest of the day.

Shimoda couldn't understand why he had failed the test.

Anyway, he returned at a later date and bragged he was passed on the spot. This time no road test was required. Nobody wanted to get in the car with him.

Another job of mine was to interface with NSI's law firms of Sullivan & Cromwell and Kelley Drye & Warren, which was how I came to be drawn into "Operation O Canada."

One Friday afternoon in December 1976, Yukiko Murata, Egashira's secretary, left the office for the weekend. In keeping with the mysterious ways of the Japanese, she never bothered to tell anyone that her visa was about to expire and that she had done nothing to renew it. She received a notice to leave the United States by a certain date, and so she did. She thought all she had to do was go to Canada for the weekend, get a renewal, and return on Sunday. That would put her back at her desk on Monday morning without anyone being the wiser.

Once Miss Murata arrived in Montreal, things began to go very wrong. The U.S. consul general didn't see the situation quite the way she did, and she was refused a new visa. She was fortunate she was even allowed to remain in Montreal and not deported to Tokyo by the Canadians.

Even though "Ellie," as she was to rename herself, was just a secretary at Nomura, she was still the daughter of Munetada Murata, who was vice chairman of the parent company and would eventually become chairman. Therefore, Ellie's woes were taken very seriously indeed in the New York offices.

Ellie very much didn't want to be sent back to Japan. Few unattached Japanese women, having tasted the freedom of the Western world, want to return to their homeland. It was said her father had no control over her impulsive ways and wasn't happy with the thought of seeing her back home, either.

NSI's senior management dropped everything, and all efforts were directed to retrieving Ellie from Montreal. Operation O Canada was put into high gear. Nomura called in high-priced Sullivan & Cromwell to handle this hot potato. Margaret Blomquist, an associate, was given the assignment. She later admitted to me she was appalled by the NSI claims. Miss Murata suddenly became a "brevet" vice president. NSI told Mrs. Blomquist that the company was powerless to conduct its business activities without Miss Murata, practically to the point of not being able to open the front door unless Miss Murata turned the key. Mrs. Blomquist was even more amazed that the Immigration Service swallowed the fishy story. But the fact is, even though the consul general in Montreal was highly skeptical, the U.S. government in Washington accepted the tale hook, line, and sinker. Miss Murata was allowed back. However, the NASD reports that the FBI deported her in early 1982 for unknown reasons. Like a boomerang, she again returned several years later.

Along with all these other shenanigans, I had to keep watch over vendors. In a large company, taking care of office supplies would fall into the province of the purchasing agent. NSI wasn't that large yet, so the job became one of my part-time duties. I dealt with a wide array of people, handling everything from paper for the Xerox machine to coffee and soft drinks for the vending machines.

For a crooked person, it was a license to steal. Even I, pretty hardened to Wall Street's manipulations, was surprised by the shifty practices that companies employed to hawk their products. Their standard procedure was to contact the person ordering the company's supplies and bribe him. I would answer the phone and hear the same opening line again and again: "Hi, John, what's your home address?"

Even though I knew what was coming after the first experience, I always played it the same way. "Why do you want to know?" I would ask.

"Well, we want to get to know you and open an account with Nomura" would come the reply. "We're sending you a nineteen-inch color TV [or microwave oven or set of golf clubs or Tahiti vacation] to show our appreciation."

That's known as bribery. Other times, I was offered a "cash discount." Hand-delivered in a plain envelope. That's known as a kickback.

Everybody got the same answer: "I don't do business that way." Then I would go on to say, "We already have established vendors who have been with us for years. We feel loyal to them. However, if your product is competitive in price and in quality, then let's talk."

Rarely did they feel like talking, and so rarely were new accounts opened.

Later on, someone else got my job as purchasing agent. One day I happened to encounter him in a hallway in front of a rarely used closet. The closet doors were wide open, and I noticed the closet was crammed with cases of light bulbs. The office used overhead fluorescent lights, yet these were bulbs for table lamps. What's more, NSI wasn't responsible for the lights. The building management replaced them when they burned out. Yet there were enough bulbs in there to light up Madison Square Garden.

13

Buyer Beware

IT MADE A LOT OF SENSE FOR NSI TO SET UP AND RUN AN American investment fund. That was a sure way to make some real money. But knowing what I did about the abilities of the Japanese, I dreaded to think how that might go. I found out in September 1976.

That month, the Nomura Capital Fund of Japan was born when 3,165,529 shares of stock were offered to American investors at $10 a share. By no means was this the first Japanese fund made available in the United States. The Japan Fund was. But the Nomura Capital Fund was the first real mutual fund sponsored by a Japanese firm. Nomura was the comanager of the deal, but in name only. Merrill Lynch, the other comanager, sold the shares. Nevertheless, the Nomura people were breaking their arms patting their own backs for the fabulous job they had done. But as time went on, there turned out to be a little bit more to the story.

The fund's gestation actually went back some years, when Merrill Lynch and Nomura came to an agreement to launch a two-part plan involving Merrill and its investment advisory firm, Lionel D. Edie, and Nomura and its investment company, Nomura Capital Management. The first step was for Nomura Tokyo to sell a newly created American mutual fund to its Japanese clients. The fund was called FundAmerica of Japan. Merrill Lynch would serve as cosponsor, and Lionel D. Edie would act as the investment advisor and portfolio manager. FundAmerica was born on April 12, 1973. The initial buyers were Japanese clients of Nomura, who invested about $32.4

million of their hard-earned dollars. Unfortunately, this sum never grew any larger, but instead started a downhill slide into oblivion.

A weekly report of FundAmerica's activities was distributed within NSI. (At most Wall Street houses, such facts were considered inside information, but because NSI wasn't directly involved, nobody cared.) Judging from the types of stocks in the fund, the portfolio manager must have been under the heavy influence of the Growth Stock Theory of the 1960s. According to the growth theory, you could buy just about any high-priced stock and sell it at a still higher price. In other words, it was the Greater Fool Theory: If you were foolish enough to buy an overpriced stock, you could always sell it to someone even more foolish. One of the key stocks in the FundAmerica portfolio was Avon Products, a star from the growth stock era that was about to take a terrifying nosedive. It plunged from a high of $130 to $23 by the fall of 1974. That's what happens to greater fools. By July 1981 the few remaining shares of FundAmerica would be quietly redeemed, and the fund died a silent death.

The second step of the plan hatched by Nomura and Merrill Lynch was the mirror image of FundAmerica—the Nomura Capital Fund of Japan, which would enable Americans to invest in the Japanese stock market. As part of the agreement, Nomura sent one of its employees to the Tokyo office of Merrill Lynch to act as an advisor. Lionel D. Edie in turn supplied a representative for NSI in New York, John C. Quinn.

Quinn arrived in early 1976 and quickly picked up the nickname "Golden Boy." One reason was his curly blond hair, and the other was that Egashira thought the sun rose and set in him. John was extraordinarily smart; he had graduated from Yale, and while on loan to NSI, he completed his doctorate in international law. NSI's management was so taken with him, in fact, that it began to treat him as if he were truly part of the company. I was told to order business cards for John identifying him as an NSI vice president, even though he was never employed by Nomura. I got worried enough about the legalities of this that I contacted a partner in NSI's law firm, who agreed with me that it could not be done. I passed this advice on to the chief of NSI's administration department, Kiyoshi

Kobayashi. He nodded his understanding. I heard nothing more on the subject until some time later when I saw Quinn passing out an NSI card showing him as a vice president. He was the first *gaijin* to have the flip side of his business card in Japanese. Before, it was only for the Nomura people.

To make matters worse, Nomura went ahead and listed Quinn in the prospectus of the Nomura Capital Fund of Japan as an NSI vice president "from 1976 to present." In actuality, Quinn's main function at NSI had little to do with the fund. Rather, he was working in the institutional sales department, even though he was not licensed to do so. He couldn't be. He was not employed by NSI.

When Quinn arrived, Nomura was in the early stages of setting up its Nomura Capital Management division to run the new fund. One of his first assignments was to hire a mutual fund management company expert. That's when I got dragged in, since I was the personnel manager, and I helped recruit John Frederick Wallace. Once he came aboard, the creation of Nomura Capital Management went like clockwork. I found space for the operation at 100 Wall Street, which was quickly furnished; if nothing else, NSI had plenty of surplus furniture. Whenever somebody from the Tokyo staff was recalled to Japan, the company automatically bought his apartment furniture since, for some reason I never quite figured out, the man's replacement always bought new furniture. We had enough couches and tables lying around to think about getting into competition with Levitz.

Next we needed to hire a portfolio manager. Alfred N. Coleman III, who had been working in Nomura's San Francisco office, volunteered for the job. He seemed a perfect candidate. Besides having held several positions in portfolio management with a number of other companies, he had been dealing in Japanese stocks for two years at NSI.

Coleman said he took his time and carefully constructed a sound portfolio of Japanese securities that would be likely to produce good appreciation for American shareholders. Before long, however, he began to complain that Egashira and Hitoshi Tonomura, an unlicensed senior vice president at NSI, were exerting undue pressure on him. It seems they didn't like his results—not the performance of the fund, which was good, but the lack of commissions generated for NSI. It became clear to Coleman that the purpose of the fund, as far as NSI was concerned, was to serve as a cash cow that could be milked for commission business. The interests of the American shareholders were of no particular concern to NSI's management.

As if the local pressure on him weren't bad enough, Coleman claimed Tokyo also jumped on his back. It wanted to use the fund's portfolio as a dumping ground for its trading mistakes, a sort of financial landfill. Plainly put, the idea was to stick American investors with rotten trades and thus enable Japanese clients to escape losses.

The one thing the unwary Americans had going for them was Fred Coleman. He was a man of honor with a strong enough will to ward off the Japanese pressure. At least for a while. After fourteen months, however, the Japanese grew exasperated and dismissed Coleman for "unsatisfactory" performance. This despite the fact that in 1977, when the Dow Jones average finished with a loss of 20.2 percent, the Nomura Capital Fund was down just 5.6 percent. In the first quarter of 1978 the Lipper Analytical Service, which monitors mutual funds, singled out the Nomura fund as its number-one performer. For its prior twelve months, it was up 24.8 percent while the Dow Jones was off 3.7 percent. Some unsatisfactory performance! Most Wall Street firms would pay a handsome premium to get it.

Taking over for Coleman was Nobuo Katayama, a dyed-in-the-wool Nomura man who was born to follow orders. He liked to go by his Christian name, Luke, which led some of us to refer to him as "Cool Hand Luke." Once he settled in, a bamboo curtain descended around his office, and very little ever leaked out about what he was up to. One thing that eventually became clear was a markedly different track record for the fund. In *Forbes* magazine's June 1979 listing of the performance of 630 mutual funds, the Nomura Capital Fund ranked fourth from the bottom. At the end of the year, Lipper put it 475th out of the 479 funds it monitored. And yet as far as anyone could tell, management was pleased with Cool Hand Luke.

However, things got worse and worse, until in May 1980 the fund passed from the financial pages into the obituaries. Its market value had sunk to less than $8 million from its peak of $31 million. Merrill Lynch came riding to the rescue, took over the management of the fund, and renamed it the Merrill Lynch Pacific Fund. By the end of 1989 the fund's assets had swollen to $318 million. Its average annual total return amounted to 33.7 percent, and its performance record was legendary (though it did take a drubbing like all other mutual funds in the wake of the 1987 stock market crash).

Fred Coleman wound up returning to the Pacific Northwest, where he became a highly successful senior portfolio manager. And Cool Hand Luke? He was recalled to Tokyo, where he was appointed the portfolio manager for the $94 million Nomura Pacific Fund.

It was finally beginning to dawn on Nomura, as well as on the other Japanese firms, that Wall Street was inherently a service industry and that the American marketplace was of a vastly different complexion than its beloved Kabuto-cho. By the late 1970s, after twenty years of trying to make headway, much of their investment was still going straight down the tubes. A change of strategy was in order. Wall Street wasn't likely to alter the way it operated, so the Japanese needed to run some new plays. Accordingly, Nomura decided it ought to make direct investments in American-owned and -run companies.

It would buy a sizable stake of an American broker, retain the American management to run the operation, and meanwhile, Japanese trainees would be absorbed into the company to learn the ropes. The thinking was, "Today's trainees will be tomorrow's professionals and next week's managers."

Nomura had actually been involved in an aborted attempt to buy into the forerunner of Shearson Lehman Hutton back in 1973. At the time, the firm was known as CBWL Hayden Stone. Lou Riggio, who had been authorized to explore investments in New York Stock Exchange firms, had identified Hayden Stone as a good prospect and opened negotiations. Within short order, rough terms were agreed to: Nomura would pay $10 million for a one-third interest. At the time, foreign interest in a NYSE firm was restricted to 25 percent, but there was a way around that. The Nomura investment would be in the form of convertible bonds, not a direct equity investment. Since Nomura expected the NYSE to liberalize its rules eventually and abandon its barrier against foreign membership, it hoped ultimately to convert the bonds into stock.

With everything basically settled, Tokyo dispatched a delegation of senior Nomura officials to New York to wrap up the deal. Although Riggio had been the key negotiator throughout, he was not invited to the final meeting because he wasn't a member of the parent company. Somehow, behind those closed doors, some funny things happened. Incredibly, Nomura demanded that it wanted an equity interest, not convertible bonds, and refused to budge from this new stance. Hayden Stone said it couldn't possibly comply. If it did, it would have to withdraw from the NYSE. Nomura thus blew the chance of a lifetime. As time passed, Hayden Stone became Shearson Lehman Hutton, one of the mightiest firms on Wall Street. Nomura's $10 million stake would have become a fortune too big to count, and it might today be the biggest U.S. investment banker.

Sorely disappointed that the Shearson deal fell through, Nomura was determined not to let it happen again. In February 1977, opportunity number two came knocking on the door. It came walking out in the form of a report that Egashira had asked Mr. T's information services department to draw up on the American brokerage industry. This time the chance wasn't going to slip through Nomura's fingers.

Egashira was especially interested in the consolidation of Wall Street firms and the ills of the research boutiques, the small brokerage firms that specialized in securities research. Ever since the NYSE had abolished fixed commission rates on May 1, 1975, the money to pay for research had been evaporating, and the days of the research boutiques were numbered.

By now Johnson and Ruff had been fired, and Lou Riggio was in Terada's department. He got stuck doing the work. Terada had promised Egashira that the report would be finished in a day. Riggio went berserk when he heard that.

"No problem, Lou-san," Terada said. "I have material right here."

And he did. He had stacks and stacks of paper piled all over his desk, under his desk, in filing cabinets, on top of tables, everywhere but hanging from the light fixtures. The two of them worked into the evening patching together a lengthy report. Despite the impossible schedule, they produced an excellent document. Egashira praised it highly.

The report, not surprisingly, was rather harsh on the research-oriented firms on the Street. That advice notwithstanding, NSI soon entered into discussions with H. C. Wainwright, a small old Boston firm that catered to the carriage trade of Boston society. As it happened, Wainwright was in the midst of splitting the company into two entities: one to service individual investors, and the other to handle institutional clients. NSI's interest was in the latter, a firm top-heavy with analysts and with virtually no capital to support the operations.

Wainwright's president, Alfred Morley, was from the institutional side of Wall Street and had nothing to do with his company's retail sales. According to Morley, the institutional efforts produced almost 90 percent of the firm's revenues and all of its profits. Therefore the institutional partners wanted a split.

From the start, it was patently obvious that Wainwright's institutional division was grossly undercapitalized. It boasted a staff of thirty-three well-known analysts. This constellation of research stars was supported by $3 million in capital. The average salary and bonus for these guys was more than $100,000 per star, a pretty princely sum in the 1970s. The problem was getting paid by the institutional clients.

Institutions normally pay brokers for services through a chit system. If a broker gave a hot tip to a money manager and the manager made money off the recommendation, then the money manager would draw up a payment request, or "chit," which he would hand to his trading desk, requesting that the desk direct commissions to the broker. There was a priority list, however, and only so many dollars to go around. Often there wasn't enough to cover the entire stack of chits, so some brokers didn't get their money.

During a weak stock market, these research chits pile up like confetti in Times Square on New Year's Eve. Eventually they are vacuumed up, and the smaller firms never get paid a cent. Wainwright fell into this hard-luck category. In 1976 the stock market plateaued before slipping into a protracted decline the following year. Volume fell, and there wasn't enough business to pay off the large brokers, let alone the smaller ones. Wainwright needed help in a big way.

In late 1976 H. C. Wainwright's institutional division actually saw its volume of business expanding, but its expenses were also rising. Due to changes in the brokerage business and the drop in commission rates, Wainwright's revenue base was declining. Morley said it was only a matter of time before the expense and revenue lines would be crossing. The company was in trouble and open for a merger.

Riggio had read in the paper that Wainwright was scouting about for a friendly merger partner, so he tipped off Wainwright that NSI might be receptive. At the same time, Egashira had sought out the advice of Wally Stern of Capital Research concerning a joint venture between NSI and an American firm. Stern told Alfred Morley of Nomura's interest.

Morley had several meetings with Egashira, and the pieces began falling into place. The Japanese Ministry of Finance gave its blessing, and Wainwright's management sat down with Egashira, Kurokawa, and several others from Tokyo. A deal was struck in February 1977. Nomura paid $1 million for a 24.9 percent stake in Wainwright Securities.

The investment in Wainwright seemed sensible. It opened the doors to business between the two firms' client bases. NSI gained access to WSI's nine hundred clients and Wainwright to Nomura's foreign customers. Neither, however, was able to capitalize on this edge. WSI's business continued to expand, but unfortunately, so did its expenses—and at a much faster clip. By the summer of 1977 WSI needed more money, namely about a million bucks. Egashira, however, refused to pump in any more, and WSI even turned to the investment banking firm of Dillon Read for help, but an acceptable deal couldn't be arranged.

Given the direction that the brokerage business was headed, toward trading and away from research, I felt NSI's joint venture was doomed from the start. By summer this was clear to just about everyone. So I buttonholed Riggio and said, "Lou, you got NSI into this mess, now it's time to get us out."

"How?" he said.

"Let's sell it to Blyth Eastman Dillon," I replied.

Riggio said, "Nobody could be dumb enough to buy Wainwright!"

But I felt otherwise. Blyth, which would itself eventually be acquired by Paine Webber, had gotten nowhere in doing business with NSI. Its New York international salesman would jog naked down Wall Street for the opportunity. So I told Lou, "Approach the BED salesman and tell him there's an opportunity for BED to buy WSI. The advantages far outweigh the disadvantages. In acquiring WSI, BED will have its pick of thirty-three top-flight research analysts for its own department. Next, it will be forming an association with Nomura Securities. This association will produce a bridge to the Orient for BED and all its products, especially its investment banking division. And naturally, BED's salesman will be in position to get the lion's share of Nomura's stock exchange commission business. That'll appeal to him. The best part of it all, it will not cost Blyth anything!"

I figured that the INA Corporation, an insurance holding company that was Blyth's parent, could simply turn on its printing presses and run off treasury stock to buy Wainwright. It would probably take about eighty-five thousand shares, then worth about $45 a share, of which Nomura would get about $1 million worth.

Riggio liked the idea and took it to the Blyth salesman. He liked it too.

Then the unexpected happened. Around NSI, it always did. Donald Weeden of Weeden Holding Company, a major force in what was known as the third market, abruptly entered the picture. Weeden wanted to expand its product base, and hence Weeden and Wainwright merged on October 1, 1977. The Wainwright principals got cash and convertible bonds for their WSI stock. Don Weeden offered the same deal to Nomura, but NSI, true to its old habits, demanded common stock. Weeden didn't care, and Nomura wound up with some 40,000 shares. NSI calculated the stock at book value of $25 a share, and management felt its original investment still stood at $1 million. It didn't. At the time, the stock traded at between $8 and $9 a share. So Nomura's $1 million was now worth about $350,000.

Alas, Weeden had developed some massive problems that

the Wainwright partners didn't know about, and after four months Don Weeden strolled into Morley's office and, in a rather extreme case of giving short notice, told him that the Wainwright division was to be closed the next day. Weeden itself was ultimately forced to merge yet again, joining forces with a NYSE member firm to become Moseley Hallgarten, Estabrook & Weeden, Inc.

Nomura's forty thousand shares of Weeden were exchanged for one hundred thousand shares of Moseley. They were subsequently sold in the open market for a dismaying price of 17 cents a share. Thus Nomura's $1 million investment in Wainwright Securities ended up as a measly $1,700, or about the price of a one-way ticket to Tokyo.

Not surprisingly, the debacle marked the beginning of the end of Egashira's career at Nomura. A few years later, he would leave to become president of a small Japanese trading company, J. Osawa & Co., which specialized in importing jewelry and sporting goods equipment into Japan. The company had seen better days. Its stock had once been traded on the Tokyo Stock Exchange, a great honor for a Japanese company. But some time before Egashira's arrival, it nearly crumbled into bankruptcy and its shares were delisted from the exchange.

14

Need a Honda?

ONE OF THE LASTING LEGACIES LEFT BY KEISUKE Egashira was the Monday Morning Meeting. It was conducted at eight o'clock and was ostensibly an attempt to bring the *gaijin* professionals a little further into the mainstream of Nomura. In reality, it was purely cosmetic. As soon as the meeting broke up, the Tokyo staff would go charging off to another conference room, where the real Monday Morning Meeting would be held. That one started at eight forty-five. Meanwhile, the *gaijin* would return to their desks, where they went about their duties well out of the mainstream.

During the first meeting, every department chief would have something to say. Because all were Japanese (except for the head of the syndicate department), it amounted to nothing more than a practice session for them to polish their English. It was sort of like a football scrimmage before the real game. Each of the Japanese offered a few remarks about the stupendous achievements of his section during the prior week and his bold plans for still more amazing gains in the coming week.

But by paying attention at these meetings, I was able to piece together the shady story of the Honda Motor Company underwriting of 1977.

Honda was first mentioned during the Monday meeting on June 13, 1977. Kurokawa was the moderator for the session. The fourth speaker that day was Yoshio Nitta, the unlicensed corporate finance chief, and one of the items he discussed was a forthcoming underwriting of a common stock offering from Honda. He said the company planned to file its intention with

152

the SEC on June 21. The underwriting invitations would be sent to the American underwriting firms on July 1, and the stock would be offered to investors on July 26. NSI was to be comanager, and Merrill Lynch was to be the lead manager and run the books, meaning it would allocate stock to the other members of the underwriting group for their salespeople. Vinegar Andy Saitoh noted that he would personally work on the preparation of the Honda underwriting, though, as was his custom, he didn't make clear what his efforts would consist of.

At the following week's meeting, Nitta was the first speaker. That was a sign that the coming Honda issue was now becoming an important item. Nitta said the size of the offering would be about $75 million, or roughly three million American Depository Receipts, since the stock was selling for about $25 a share. The target date for the filing was the next day, he said, but there would be no press release.

I thought this was peculiar. But Nitta explained that the Japanese Ministry of Finance wanted the news announcement to be made when the preliminary prospectus—the "red herring," so called because portions of the front page are printed in red ink—was ready. Nitta said it would be available by July 1, and the underwriting invitations would be sent at that time to the prospective underwriters. Hitoshi Tonomura, the assistant New York office manager, put in that even though the Honda issue would become public knowledge after the filing was announced, the NSI people were to "low-key" it. In other words, we weren't to talk about it.

When Vinegar Andy got his turn, he explained why we were to keep mum on the deal. The institutional sales department's plan was simple and direct. Saitoh said, "We will work on Honda and hope to sell it out in two weeks."

NSI's strategy was to get out in front of all other underwriters, who would not know about the underwriting, and presell the coming issue—prior to the filing and without benefit of the required prospectus.

In the United States, the securities laws are crystal clear on the matter of selling an underwriting. It says underwriters and members of the selling group are prohibited from discussing an issue with a prospective buyer until the buyer has a red herring in his possession. And yet a few days later, I actually caught the institutional sales department smack in the midst of a mass mailing of Honda research reports. The coordinator of the mailing was Koichi Kane, an assistant vice president who would go on to become president of Nomura International, Ltd., Nomura's giant London operation. I promptly reported my discovery to Andy Basile, the NSI compliance officer. Andy buried his face in his hands, shook his head, and said, "I don't want to hear it."

I guess he didn't, because he took no action to stop it. The next thing I knew, his superior, Jack Wallace, summoned me to his private office, motioned to a chair in front of his desk, and told me to sit down. He opened the conversation by saying, "What you thought you saw being mailed was this cover letter on the underwriting, wasn't it?" He held aloft a copy of the letter. His index finger and thumb gripped it at the top middle of the page and started jabbing it at me. He repeated, "Wasn't it?"

It did not come across as a question.

I looked him directly in the eye and said, "No! It was a research report. I know one when I see one and have written a few in my day. Those were research reports being mailed in violation of American securities laws."

Wallace just sat there and stared at me. He showed no emotion and said nothing more. The meeting ended.

The episode brought to mind a similar incident during my days in the late 1950s with Merrill Lynch in Zanesville, Ohio. Merrill was comanager of an underwriting of some Royal Dutch Petroleum stock. One of the New York offices had an overly ambitious account executive who decided to do a big sales job on the underwriting. Apparently he mailed more than two hundred of the Standard & Poor stock summary reports on Royal Dutch with a cover note. Shortly after the reports went out, the account executive's actions came to the attention of Merrill Lynch's senior management. They reported the matter to the SEC and withdrew from the underwriting. The salesman was summarily fired. It was a careless mistake, nothing more, but Merrill Lynch paid the price with the loss of tens of thousands of dollars in commissions and fees. It was also a black eye for the firm.

This time around, though, it wasn't an S & P report that was going out to buyers. It was research material coming from a managing underwriter. The report carried sales and earnings estimates and a "buy" recommendation for the stock. Not only was it illegal, but it also gave NSI a distinct advantage over its American competitors. And what made this action so serious was that it wasn't the handiwork of an isolated salesman acting on his own. It was NSI's management attempting to grab control of the Honda deal by getting a running start on the rest of its underwriting partners.

Nitta opened the June 27 Monday meeting with news about the progress of the Honda underwriting. He announced that the issue had been filed as planned on June 21, but that the invitation wires had not yet been sent. The scheduled date was July 1. The red herrings were still not ready but were expected on Friday.

In Wall Street syndicate departments, Friday is usually a mop-up day for the past week, and little business is transacted. In those days, when an underwriting invitation was issued, the recipient normally took several days to respond. The invitation usually passed through a committee or two before a decision was rendered. If accepted, a member firm's syndicate department notified the rest of the firm, and upon receipt of the red herrings, a sales effort would be mounted.

Vinegar Andy summarized what happened the week before in institutional sales, then announced the plans for the coming week. "This week we will work on the Honda issue," he said. Because NSI had already completed its mass mailing of the Honda research material, Saitoh's voice was brimming with the utmost confidence.

Several weeks later, there was one piece of news that overshadowed Honda at the Monday meeting. Kuro, the Black Bird, as some called him, was flying the coop. He announced his transfer to London and Hitoshi Tonomura's appointment as the new New York office manager. Kuro would still be around NSI until August 3, but in body only. In American companies when people are transferred, there is a transition period. Within Nomura, there is none. The person being transferred drops all duties and responsibilities immediately. It was strange for me to see yesterday's hard-working executive now sitting in the employees' lounge, smoking a cigarette and gazing into space with nothing at all to do.

The meeting returned to business. Nitta was visiting Atlanta on the Honda deal, so there were no comments from him. However, Haruo Miyako, the assistant manager of the syndicate department, had some remarks. He opened his report by mentioning that the previous week's key issue had been a Dow Chemical bond offering. The underwriting was in serious trouble. Miyako said it had gotten off to a promising start, but an electrical failure by Consolidated Edison (the blackout of 1977) had also short-circuited the bond market. Prices collapsed and buyers vanished. NSI was stuck with an inventory problem of $800,000 in unsold bonds and a falling bond market.

NSI was also staring at another inventory problem: the coming Honda offering. The pricing was ten days away, and NSI had five hundred thousand ADRs to sell—and even with its unfair start, it had relatively few buyers in sight. Miyako said the offering date has been set for the following Tuesday, and of NSI's 800,000 shares, the company had sold 300,000. His math was slightly off. Only 200,000 shares had been sold. He gave this breakdown: The Honolulu office had sold 50,000; San Francisco 60,000; Los Angeles 50,000; and New York had orders for 40,000 from institutions.

At one of the earlier meetings, which I had missed, Saitoh had explained why NSI had such a huge number of shares for sale. It was for no shallow motive. Merrill Lynch had been signed up as a comanager of the deal, and Merrill had sold 800,000 shares. NSI wanted to show Merrill that it too had the stuff it took to sell that amount.

At the time, Merrill had a capital base of $662 million, 269 domestic offices, and 6,100 salesmen. All told, the firm employed 20,415 people. By contrast, NSI had capital of $15 million, 4 U.S. offices, and 15 salesmen. NSI employed a total of 89 people. And NSI was going to outsell Merrill Lynch?

Vinegar Andy's report was not at all upbeat. His plans to sell out the Honda underwriting by outflanking the rules and the other underwriters had failed. Saitoh said NSI had gotten a rather hostile reception in Chicago and Boston. As he put it, the institutional buyers had not been "too polite." That was probably a gross understatement. American automobile analysts were predicting that U.S. car sales had peaked, and all of them were hurriedly downgrading their buy recommendations for the auto industry to a hold. These were the brisk winds NSI was sailing into.

The whole deal was turning into a nightmare. Considering the circumstances, Nomura had little choice but to revise its sales approach on Honda. If the salesmen were having trouble pushing a stock, they didn't simply abandon it. Rather, they tried to make the company seem like a totally different type of enterprise. Of course, this was all done within certain limits. So the Nomura men, rather than pitching Honda as a car company, began referring to it as a "technology company" that happened to manufacture motors. Investors can be astoundingly dumb when they put their minds to it, but this silly ploy didn't work. Nobody was fooled, which probably explained why Saitoh's squad got such a testy reception. Nobody likes his intelligence insulted. A very deflated Saitoh wrapped up his report by saying, "This is the last week to sell, and we must sell five hundred thousand shares."

On Thursday Nomura pushed the panic button. Everybody in the company was recruited into a banzai-charge sales effort. Hiroshi Nagahiro, NSI's unlicensed deputy operations manager, threw his operations department into the front lines and tried to coerce his troops into selling Honda to their friends. One by one he approached every back office clerk with the same question, "Do you know any millionaires who want to buy Honda?"

He got the same reaction from all of them. The young people from the New York City high-school system sat there in total befuddlement. They were lucky if they knew someone who could afford a Honda Civic.

Friday morning, I joined the troops in the trenches. I was licensed at least, so I was legal. I twisted the arms of NSI's vendors—our insurance agent, printer, you name it—and sold several hundred shares. It was like taking a squirt gun to the Chicago fire.

No Monday morning meeting was held on July 25. The Honda issue was due to be priced the next day, and NSI had nearly 300,000 unsold shares. This was almost 10 percent of the total underwriting, and nobody had the stomach to discuss the topic.

On July 26, 3,100,000 American Depository Receipts of Honda Motor Company were officially offered to the American investors at a price of 21⅞ per share. That morning the unlicensed Tonomura represented NSI at the signing of the agreement among the underwriters. He penned his title in as "senior vice president" after his signature.

Lacking buyer interest, Honda started to fall in price. As the book runner, Merrill Lynch was forced to make a stabilizing bid on the floor of the New York Stock Exchange. By law, the book runner is the only manager permitted to support the price of a stock's underwriting, though in those days, when the book runner had to support the price of an underwriting, all the members of the selling group were required to file a Form X-17A-1 with the SEC.

The Honda underwriting was starting to look very much like a replay of the 1975 Mitsui underwriting. It was terminated on July 28, with NSI still holding 275,842 unsold shares on its inventory shelf. That represented a market value of more than $6 million. All told, NSI executed 590 orders of Honda for its clients, selling 330,458 shares in the United States. Given NSI's scanty base of operations, that in itself was a remarkable job. Then the waters started getting mighty murky.

Nomura proceeded to dispose of another 193,700 shares by illegally discounting its sales commission and "selling" them to its worldwide affiliates. The breakdown was 129,300 to Europe, 50,400 to Hong Kong, 10,000 to UBAN, and 4,000 to Singapore. These sales violated the securities rules and also afforded the Nomura overseas affiliates an unfair advantage, for they could now sell the discounted shares to foreign investors at a cheaper price than the American firms could.

By now, Nomura and NSI had grown too worried about the freefall of Honda's stock to allow laws to get in its way. Hence, on August 1, the parent sent a confidential telex to Egashira, Tonomura, and Saitoh ordering them to rig the market and support the price at 21⅛. Nomura was struggling to prop up Honda's price to avoid suffering significant underwriting losses.

As it turned out, the wire operator in Tokyo made a mistake

and sent this delicate message the regular way. Everyone at NSI read the orders. Even though the message was in Japanese, it didn't take a CIA decoder to figure out what "21⅛ *wo* maintain *shite kudsasai*" meant.

NSI gave it the old college try, enlisting the help of an unsuspecting NYSE specialist firm. The hundreds of thousands of unsold shares were transferred to NSI's trading department, where the new unlicensed department chief, Hiroshi Miyamura, took over. He had hoped to ease the stock onto the New York Stock Exchange, but its price continued to drift relentlessly lower. Since Tokyo's orders were to maintain the price at 21⅛, he was forced to buy instead of sell, and NSI's inventory of Honda stock ballooned. At this juncture, the New York team was in hopeless shape, so Nomura Tokyo came to the rescue.

It was stated in the prospectus that these shares were not registered in Japan. To offer and sell them there would violate Japanese securities laws. But Nomura Tokyo paid the laws no heed. I managed to get a look at NSI's internal records, which showed that the unsold American shares were converted from the ADRs into Japanese shares, and according to what I heard around NSI, the parent dumped the shares onto the Tokyo Stock Exchange.

A few days later, Lou Riggio called this to the attention of Terada. "Terada-san, isn't this illegal, and isn't Nomura selling unregistered stock in Japan?" he asked. He handed Mr. T a copy of the final prospectus. Terada shot Riggio a pained look. He had nothing to say.

On August 3 Ben Goodly, NSI's syndicate manager, dutifully filed the required report on the underwriting with the SEC. The figure he reported, however, did not quite jibe with Nomura's internal reports. Goodly actually had the audacity to claim that NSI had oversold its underwriting position by fourteen hundred shares.

Merrill Lynch had, in fact, oversold its underwriting, a normal and perfectly legal practice for a book runner, and needed two hundred thousand shares to help cover its short position. A highly reliable source at Merrill told me that they knew NSI had unsold shares and beseeched NSI several times for the return of the stock. NSI refused, because it would have had to give back the selling commission as well. Thus Merrill was compelled to go into the open market and buy the necessary stock. That, of course, is exactly what NSI figured it would have to do. This would enable NSI to sell back to Merrill its unsold underwriting shares at a profit and, with Merrill's open market buying, keep Honda's price at 21⅛ as Tokyo had ordered.

I was growing increasingly uncomfortable with the irregularities at Nomura, but I didn't really know what to do. The right thing, of course, would be to blow the whistle. But I was interested in preserving my own scalp. I wasn't independently wealthy, and the code on Wall Street dictates that a whistle blower is a pariah. Future employment on the Street becomes impossible. Even if I kept my mouth shut, I doubted I could get another job quickly, because the market was just too tight. I also figured that if Nomura kept fooling around, the regulatory authorities were bound to find out on their own eventually and put a stop to it. The only solution that made sense to me was to stick it out and continue to report any infractions I saw to management.

Not that my tattling was leading anywhere. In the aftermath of the Honda deal, I once more told Andy Basile the grisly details of what was going on. But once again, nothing changed.

15

Down Mexico Way

By 1977 Mexico had become an item of utmost importance to the Nomura Securities Co., Ltd. The country had blossomed into a lucrative place for investment banking business. When OPEC pushed oil prices through the ceiling in the early 1970s, Mexico got stupendously rich off its new reserves (though over the years its wealth has dribbled through its fingers). The rich always need bankers to coddle them and advise them how to transform their money into still more money, so all the Japanese investment men beat a path to Mexico City, their palms outstretched. In 1972, however, Nomura managed to get the nod as the Japanese investment bankers for the country. This achievement was largely due to the diligence and skill of Lou Riggio, who spent untold amounts of time in the country negotiating on Nomura's behalf. Riggio was a stellar pitchman, and the Mexicans were eager to displace the *gringos*, meaning American firms, to the greatest extent as possible. Once a company had grabbed the lead position, Nomura began to reap the spoils. In time, it persuaded the Mexican government to raise capital in Japan by issuing several yen-denominated bond offerings. Because the principal and the interest were payable in yen, these bonds were called, in Wall Street lingo, samurai bonds.

The first Mexican samurai bond issue, 10 billion yen worth of bonds, was bestowed on a smiling Nomura in 1973. The second issue, another 10 billion yen worth, came to market in 1976, and it too was bestowed on Nomura. As it happened, there was a new twist added the second time around. Nomura's archrival, Daiwa Securities, had been slipped in as comanager of the deal. For whatever reason, this development went totally unnoticed by the Nomura staff and didn't seem to faze anybody in the slightest. Riggio had been dumped into syndicate sales and couldn't do anything about it. Besides, the sands of time on his NSI career were running out and he was probably a few months away from being dismissed, so he had no interest in any developments down Mexico way. Then, in June 1977, Mexico filed for a record 20 billion yen offering in Japan. Something was terribly wrong with the financing. To Nomura's shock and acute embarrassment, Daiwa was appointed the lead manager. It was a tremendous coup for Japan's second-ranked investment bankers and a devastating loss of face for Nomura.

Nomura largely had itself to blame for this turn of events. The fact that Daiwa had been eased into the second samurai underwriting as a comanager should have set off some pretty loud alarms. But instead, Tokyo continued to think that Nomura's grip on Mexico was as ironclad as ever, and no one had bothered to fortify Riggio's early inroads. This threw the door wide open for Nomura's eager competitors.

Egashira was forced to take charge and try to solve this thorny problem. At the parent's behest, he plucked Riggio from his exile in NSI's information services department and hurriedly dispatched him to Mexico City. The man Egashira and Kuro had earlier tried to sack was now expected to save the day for them, after they had neglected this vital account for nearly two years.

Riggio's arrival in Mexico City was timed to meet a Nomura delegation jetting in from Tokyo. It consisted of Yukio Aida, the dynamic chief of the international department, and his assistant, Kanju Sugimoto. In the wake of the scandals that rocked the Japanese brokerage industry in 1991 (payback of securities losses to selected large clients and dealings with the "Godfather" of Japan's underworld), Nomura Securities called the sixty-seven-year-old Aida out of retirement and named him "honorary" chairman. In 1977, even though Aida was on an emergency mission to try to recoup some lost ground for Nomura, Aida seemed more concerned about his comfort. Riggio had booked them into the María Isabel Sheraton, one of the nicer hotels, but Aida was unhappy because the drawing room was too small. He also complained about the quality of Mexican wine.

One of their first meetings was with Alejandro Morales de la Vega, submanager of the Banco Nacional de Mexico. Morales told the group he had not heard from Nomura in a while, during which Daiwa had assiduously courted the Mexican officials.

More meetings followed with other Mexican officials, but everything the Japanese heard corroborated what Morales had told them. After that, there really wasn't too much that could be done, so Aida returned to Japan and left Riggio and Sugimoto to try to recover some lost territory.

It was not until a meeting with Alfredo del Mazo, the public debt director for the Mexican Ministry of Finance, and Manuel Ransom, the subdirector of markets and a man of considerable clout, that some true light began to be shed on Nomura's problem in Mexico.

Del Mazo was about forty-five minutes late for the session, so Ransom held court. To the surprise of the Nomura delegation, Ransom mentioned that he was an expert on the Tokyo capital markets and claimed credit for choosing Daiwa to be the lead manager in the coming underwriting. Ransom added that his government had no complaint with Nomura's performance in past financings, but he felt a rotation of managers would best serve his country. He claimed credit for getting Nomura displaced as the nation's exclusive Japanese investment banker. Ransom filled the wait for del Mazo with Daiwa propaganda. When del Mazo finally arrived, he confirmed that he had accepted Ransom's recommendation to use the services of Daiwa. Riggio and Sugimoto exchanged glances. Riggio became suspicious. Why was Ransom so gung ho on Daiwa?

A number of additional meetings were held in an attempt to increase interest in Nomura, but Sugimoto seemed distracted. Almost with each passing hour, he had become more and more somber, and his eyes became set in a permanent squint. He didn't voice any complaint, so Riggio let it pass, until at one session he saw that Sugimoto's face had become almost beet red, and a tear glistened on his cheek. He knew Sugimoto was unhappy about the lost business, but to this extent? It turned out that the Japanese executive was afflicted by a serious dental abcess. With his mouth practically exploding in pain, Sugimoto confessed that Nomura's regular dentist had patched up the abcess and advised him that the job would hold together for the duration of the Mexico trip. Unfortunately, it hadn't. Well, let's find another dentist, Riggio said. But Sugimoto stubbornly refused until the next day. When the dentist wondered why he had endured the excruciating pain so long, Sugimoto replied, "I didn't know there were any dentists in Mexico."

After a week, Riggio returned to New York, and Sugimoto, his mouth pain-free once again, went back to Tokyo. In keeping with company policy, Riggio filed a detailed report covering all the meetings and sent it to Japan. But he didn't put quite everything he knew into that report. He saved something for a confidential letter that he sent to Sugimoto's home. While in Mexico City, a highly placed source within the Mexican government tipped him off to check up on Manuel Ransom. When Riggio got back to New York, he did some detective work on his own and discovered that Ransom had once been employed by the Daiwa group through Daiwa Securities America, the U.S. affiliate. Ransom had joined Daiwa America in New York after receiving an MBA from the University at Albany in 1973. He worked there for more than a year before returning to his native Mexico in 1974, where he became Daiwa's most ardent supporter within the Mexican Ministry of Finance. Whenever Daiwa representatives visited Mexico, they called on Ransom first. As Riggio later put it, "It was understandable that the Nomura people came to believe Ransom was a Daiwa mole within the Mexican government."

Nomura and Riggio found themselves the beneficiaries of an incredible coincidence. One morning on or about September 1, 1977, about two and a half months after Riggio's memos went to Japan, the body of Manuel Ransom was discovered at the bottom of a stairwell, five floors beneath his Mexico City apartment. His death occurred in the middle of the night, and there were no witnesses.

I don't think for one minute that Nomura had anything to do with this accident, and there was certainly no evidence to this effect, but in short order Nomura was back in the driver's seat in Mexico, and it resumed dominance over the other Japanese brokers in Latin America in the years that ensued. To under-score this fact, Nomura received a mandate for the fourth samurai bond offering. As it happened, the principals were unable to agree on terms, and that particular issue never came to market.

Riggio was credited with pulling Nomura's chestnuts out of the Mexico fire. He was transferred back to NSI's corporate finance department and later promoted to senior vice president.

Back in New York, the more closets I poked around in at NSI, the more skeletons I discovered. One day I learned from some colleagues that on February 6, 1976, NSI had its lawyer, Martin Budd of Sullivan & Cromwell, write to the SEC to ask a favor. In Wall Street jargon, what Nomura wanted was a "no-action letter." When a brokerage firm wants to engage in specific securities transactions it believes are not covered under the rules and regulations, it requests a no-action letter from the SEC. The broker will lay out what it wishes to do and request that the SEC take no legal action against the broker. If the SEC approves the proposal, it will issue the no-action letter. It's akin to asking a village constable, "Is it okay to jaywalk across a dirt road if no cars are coming?" and getting the reply, "Yes, if it's a dirt road and there are no cars coming."

Budd's letter asked the SEC to allow NSI to sell Japanese foreign bills of exchange even though these securities were not registered with the SEC, as required by the Securities Act of 1933. These short-term treasury bills, maturing in sixty days, were issued by the Japanese government and underwritten by Japanese brokers.

The SEC replied that the bills could not be issued without compliance with the law. In short, no way, pal. But NSI didn't let rejections get in its way. It completely ignored the adverse ruling and inundated the United States with these unregistered securities. Many might consider that as serious an offense as any broker can commit, especially since it asked for and got an SEC opinion in advance.

To market the bills, NSI devised a clever scheme. Because the bills fell under the heading of underwritings, the task of masterminding this scam fell to Hitoshi Tonomura (who would eventually be promoted to executive managing director of the Tokyo parent and put in charge of Nomura's international operations). He was an appropriate choice, since he wasn't licensed. So we had NSI's unregistered senior vice president orchestrating the sale of Japan's unregistered treasury bills.

Essentially, the ploy was a play on the foreign currency markets and interest rates. It was a two-part deal. For American investors, the first step was the purchase of the bills. The second step was a hedging operation in the currency markets. The bills were sold at a slight discount from their redemption price and redeemed at face value in sixty days. The difference produced a yield of about 4 percent. Because the American investors had to pay yen for the bills, they needed to convert their dollars into the Japanese currency. At the end of the sixty days, they had to change the yen back into dollars. To avoid being affected by any unfavorable fluctuation in the foreign currency markets, they would hedge, that is, purchase a futures contract guaranteeing a fixed rate of exchange at the end of the sixty-day period. At the time, the yen was strong and the dollar was selling at a 5.8 percent discount in the sixty-day futures markets. So between the bill's interest rate of 4 percent and the currency exchange profits of 5.8 percent, American investors could net a return of 9.8 percent. Not bad money, no matter how you looked at it.

At the time, American banks were borrowing money from the Federal Reserve at 6½ percent, and the major corporations were borrowing from the banks at 7¾. And yet anybody could borrow a weakening dollar, flip the dough into a riskless package of Japanese sixty-day bills plus a foreign exchange hedge, and make a pleasant profit of nearly 10 percent.

The game began in early 1977 and shifted into overdrive eleven months later, when the government of Japan, shame-faced, was forced to stop issuing the bills. By November the impact of a $4 billion inflow into the Tokyo capital markets had become disruptive. The yen soared out of control to record highs.

Late in 1977 *Business Week* carried a story headlined "Hot Money Floods the Yen." It reported that officials of the Bank of Japan, Japan's central bank, said that the sales of the bills overseas was the chief cause of the sharp rise in the yen. The article went on to say, "And ironically, it is the Big Four Japanese securities houses—Nomura, Nikko, Yamaichi, and Daiwa—that are drumming up the arbitrage business that is hurting the yen."

What quietly slipped between the cracks was NSI's rejected request for an SEC no-action letter. All of the sales in the United States were illegal. The amazing thing was how open it all was. In fact, shortly before the Japanese government suspended sales of the bills, NSI hosted an institutional bond investors' conference at a large New York hotel, drawing about a hundred and fifty people. Everyone was given a manual on how to invest in Japanese debt securities. The foreign bills of exchange were one of the featured items.

And so the curtain came down on part one of the play on interest rates. But the show wasn't over. The plot shifted to outstanding Japanese bonds maturing in sixty days. Because these securities had been issued long before, they fell under the SEC's "seasoned security rule" that applied to any securities that had been trading in foreign markets for longer than 270 days and thus were not required to be registered with the commission. The volume of this interest-rate arbitrage play soared, and the world headed for big economic trouble.

In January 1977 the yen stood at 300 to the dollar. By the end of the year it had appreciated 25 percent to 240 to the dollar. Eleven months later it hit a post–World War II high of 188 to the dollar, an increase of some 60 percent.

Granted, many factors precipitated the U.S. recession of the late 1970s and early 1980s. But a weakened dollar was the springboard that sent interest rates heading for the moon. By 1980 the prime rate skyrocketed to 21½ percent from 7¾. Inflation soared to nearly 15 percent, and unemployment climbed into the double digits.

By 1978 Japan again was forced to step in to stabilize the financial markets. This time it suspended the sale of short-term futures currency contracts and brought to a close the first post–World War II run on the dollar. Through all this hanky-panky, Nomura made it clear that it was going to do business in America one way or another. Unfortunately, that business was now coming at the expense of every American citizen.

16

Sayonara

At about 10:30 on the Tuesday morning after the Labor Day weekend in 1977, my phone rang. Keisuke Egashira wanted to see me in his office. On the face of it, there was nothing particularly unusual about that. Trying to guess what my next mission would be was fruitless.

Not long before, to cite one example of the tasks handed to me, Egashira had lost his wallet while he was visiting Paris. It contained a considerable amount of cash and $300 in traveler's checks. Since the mishap occurred on a Sunday evening, there wasn't much he could do, so he phoned the New York office and enlisted the help of his Japanese subordinates. They convened a meeting. It lasted two and a half days, and the upshot was to turn the problem over to me.

There wasn't anything I could do about the lost cash short of chasing around Paris myself looking for it, but the Citibank traveler's checks were another matter. I had a friend who was one of the bank's executive vice presidents, and I phoned him for help. I told him that one call from his secretary would probably work miracles. Sure enough, it did. The replacement checks were hand-delivered within two hours, and I was free to await my next exciting Mission Impossible.

When I walked into Egashira's office this time, however, I could tell that something was definitely amiss. Peter Pan always conducted his meetings from behind his mahogany desk, but now he was sitting regally in the chair against the window. Seated on his left was Hitoshi Tonomura. Both wore grim faces. With his right hand, Peter Pan motioned for me to sit down.

In his soft voice, he said, without preliminary remarks, "It is the decision of the executive committee that your job performance has been unsatisfactory. You will be given three months to find another job."

I was totally taken aback, even though I should have known by then that my lack of cooperation in NSI schemes left me walking on the thinnest of ice. And it was probably becoming evident to the NSI brass that I was snooping around in too many places. I gathered my wits and told Peter Pan, "I would like to see my monthly evaluation reports."

"We don't have any," he replied.

I knew that was a blatant lie. NSI made and kept quite detailed records on all its *gaijins*. By now, I had seen plenty of them in the back-office files.

I then asked, "Unsatisfactory performance in syndicate underwriting?"

"Yes."

That was a lie, as well. I had made the department the most productive and most profitable of any NSI unit, and I had the figures to prove it. Aside from a secretary and a Japanese national, I had been the only other person in the department.

"And in general affairs?" I went on.

"Yes."

That was equally absurd. Less than two years previously, I had been promoted to vice president, and in my four and a half years at Nomura, my base pay had been boosted by nearly 50 percent. This was hardly what an unsatisfactory job performance was all about.

I asked, "May I have the opportunity to face my accusers?"

"No."

I never got any further explanation, and I didn't think I would. Nobody was going to state the real reason for my being sacked, but I knew what it was all too well. It was my refusal to play along with Nomura's crooked behavior. The truth of the matter to me was pretty simple. I was fired in an attempt to discredit me and to keep me from gaining any further knowledge of Nomura's deceitful practices that I might disclose to the authorities.

Once I returned to my desk, I phoned Lou Riggio, and when he came by I gave him the news. "Oh, how stupid," he said.

"How stupid. Nomura fired the one guy who can put them out of business."

But I wasn't thinking about revenge. I was thinking about the bleak future I faced. I was forty-five years old, working in an administrative position on Wall Street for a Japanese firm. That didn't sound too great in September 1977. The Dow Jones average had topped out the year before at a then-all-time high of just over 1,000. Now it was trading in the low 800s, and Wall Street was locked in a hiring freeze. What a time to be hitting the streets.

With just three months to find a new job, I decided I'd better get hustling. I made the rounds of all the Wall Street firms and drew on every connection I had, but absolutely nothing was available. A few large brokerage firms expressed some tepid interest in me for a sales job, but I had been out of retail sales for five years and institutional sales for two, and in the end, they weren't terribly anxious to add a salesman with no clients. I even looked into an area entirely foreign to me: selling municipal bonds. I appeared for two interviews with muni houses in Jersey City, a location well known for sleazy brokerage firms, and when I showed up, I realized their reputation was probably grossly understated. The trading room at the first was peopled by guys who looked like thugs plucked out of dark alleys. I kept plugging away, but things seemed grim. With every passing day, I felt more disconsolate and more embittered.

I tried hard to get some interviews in the corporate syndicate area, the specialty in which I had really shone at NSI. But I couldn't get in the door anywhere. I was sending out ten to fifteen résumés a day, and nothing was coming back. I found out why a little later. A headhunter I had been working with told me, "Everybody knew there were funny things going on at Nomura, and they thought you were a part of them. So nobody would touch you with a ten-foot pole. They didn't know you were clean."

Before I reached the point of seeing about selling apples on a street corner or training to become a barber, Dick Gibson, one of NSI's syndicate salesmen, asked me out for drinks and told me he had heard that a small Japanese broker, Nippon Kangyo

Kakumaru, was starting an underwriting department. "I know you've had a bellyful of the Japanese," he said, "but why not look into it?"

And so I did. Unfortunately, I was two weeks late. The firm had already hired another *gaijin* to head its syndicate department. Not knowing what else to do, I started pitching myself to the other Japanese brokers in town, including the newest one to open its doors, Sanyo Securities, which, it turned out, was also launching a syndicate department. I had four or five meetings with the Sanyo people over several weeks. They kept me on edge, but they hired me.

There was one bizarre irony in this. Sanyo, as it happens, is one-third owned by Nomura. You can bet that if someone got fired from the Buick division of General Motors, there would be no way the person would ever get hired by Chevrolet. I received an offer from Sanyo, but almost lost my job as soon as I got it. The hiring process proceeded smoothly enough, and I reported to work for Sanyo on January 3, 1978, as a vice president. It is routine procedure on Wall Street, however, to verify the past employment of all new hires. Accordingly, Sanyo sent the standard questionnaire to NSI. The form was addressed to Andy Basile. What came back was a beauty of a hatchet job signed by Jack Wallace.

When I got wind of the report, I hurriedly hired a lawyer to protect myself. He wrote a letter to NSI charging "wrongful termination of employment." Some months later, the action resulted in a meeting between a partner of Kelley, Drye & Warren, NSI's lawyers, and me. During our session, I brought up three examples of NSI's irregular behavior: the company's failure to register supervisory personnel, Ben Goodly's two unlicensed syndicate salesmen, and the Honda underwriting scam.

Not surprisingly, the NSI lawyer dismissed all three charges as trifling, as if they were no more important than having put out the garbage on the wrong day. His answers might well have been swallowed by someone who didn't work on Wall Street and know its nuances, but not by those in the investment industry. On the matter of NSI's failure to license supervisory personnel, he said, "Nomura assured me that they have at least eleven registered principals at any one time, and you should not concern yourself because this wasn't your responsibility." The NASD manual, of course, makes it clear that *all* supervisors must be registered. A securities license is not an umbrella license any more than a driver's license is. As for the two syndicate salesmen, the lawyer said one salesman was hired before the expiration of his license and the other had misrepresented himself to Nomura. The latter, he added, was terminated upon discovery. But NSI's own records showed a later starting date for the first salesman than he cited. And the other salesman had never misrepresented himself; we discovered he was not licensed the day he started selling for NSI. The man had in fact been fired, but for altogether different reasons. A customer of his had reneged on a trade that went sour, costing NSI $10,000; when his superior told him he would have to eat the loss, he refused and was dismissed. Finally, the partner said that Kelley, Drye & Warren would advise NSI to refile a "corrected" report to the SEC on the Honda deal. I doubt if they did it. It had already been more than a year since Ben Goodly had signed the original. And the lawyer's willingness spoke for itself: if nothing was wrong, why was it necessary to refile?

My lawyer had asked for my job back, or, failing that, some sort of restitution. Both were refused. What I did get from NSI was a vow not to make any more comments about me, good or bad. The lawyer, however, also gave me some further unsolicited advice. As I was heading out the door from our meeting, he told me in passing, "If you blow the whistle on Nomura, you'll be a marked man for life. So don't do it."

His advice came out of the blue. I had said nothing whatsoever about exposing NSI. Obviously, the possibility was uppermost in his mind.

I looked at him, said nothing, and continued walking.

I joined Sanyo as a vice president. My initial job was to get its underwriting department off the ground. Sanyo set two primary goals for me: Take no losses, and be competitive with our peers, the other second-tier Japanese firms such as New Japan Securities, Kankaku Securities, and Wako Securities. To take on any of Japan's Big Four brokerage houses would be sheer fantasy.

Setting up a syndicate department was something I knew how to do, but it was no easy task. One of the last things Wall Street needed was another Japanese stockbroker trying to become an American underwriter. Yet I had a useful tool to work with: Sanyo's daily order flow of American stocks from Tokyo. Because Sanyo was not a New York Stock Exchange member, all of its orders were doled out to American securities firms. The parent bought and sold thousands of shares of American stock for its Japanese clients. It had been fervently promoting the "buy America" concept in Japan with good success.

Sanyo's management arranged a peculiar intraoffice policy for distributing those orders. The ones that arrived on Mondays, Wednesdays, and Fridays would be placed by the Japanese stock section. Those guys were trying hard to attract Japanese stock orders from American brokers that Sanyo could then execute in Tokyo. I was handed the Tuesday and Thursday orders to try to secure underwriting invitations from the Wall Street investment bankers.

Sometimes I got other types of offers for my stock business. One American stockbroker offered to split his commission take with me; I turned him down. Another told me: "If there is anything you want, I can get it for you." He was famous among the Japanese as "the Entertainment King." He even rented an apartment on the Upper East Side. I had heard there was a two-week wait for the key. I was easier to please. I only wanted his firm to put Sanyo into its underwritings. And I got my wish.

Within a couple of years, things picked up nicely. I managed to make Sanyo a big enough factor to rank just below Japan's Big Four. In 1988 I even succeeded in moving us into first place among the Japanese in underwriting stocks. In time, I was assigned additional responsibilities. The management discontinued its Monday-Wednesday-Friday rotation policy and put me in charge of executing its daily American securities orders. I was made a senior vice president.

While I immersed myself in my new job, I can't say I put Nomura behind me. My experiences at NSI tugged at me, and I continued to keep an eye on what the firm was up to.

The company did lie fairly low for the next few years. In the fall of 1985, however, it made another move, one that carried it to the very top of the mountain. It applied to become a primary dealer of American government securities.

A major function of the New York Federal Reserve Bank is to oversee the U.S. government securities markets. It designates a select few brokers as primary dealers of the securities and deals only with them in open market operations. These primary dealers basically make the market for all government and Treasury bonds and set the tone and pace of what is the world's largest securities market. In short, they act as Uncle Sam's investment bankers.

Being a primary dealer allows a firm to sell such issues to investors at the lowest possible price. In fact, some large institutions insist on doing business only with the primary dealers. In short, a dealership can be a wonderful way to make eye-popping profits. In 1986, for instance, the twenty-two primary dealers carved up income of $2 billion. Several years later, when the field was expanded to more than forty members, meaty profits became less automatic, but it was still nice to be in such exalted company.

The man responsible for Nomura's push into this market was Robin Studley Koskinen. He joined NSI in August 1984 to form its U.S. government department. I didn't meet him until much later, when he had become a legend in both the government securities markets and the American-Japanese financial community and had been widely quoted in newspapers and magazines. By that time, though, he was no longer with Nomura.

I was curious how any *gaijin* had been able to build up such an operation within NSI without its being usurped by a Japanese national. That, after all, was the usual pattern. When I asked him, he told me that when he was hired he was told he could incur as much overhead as he wished, as long as the revenues supported it. He said he had moved cautiously in building a staff and was able to recruit high-powered professionals. One was John Niehinke, a former assistant secretary of the U.S. Treasury. Koskinen said NSI's management did start getting a little edgy when he failed to hire a government bond trader until January 1985.

I didn't bother to ask Koskinen about his regulatory qualifications. After all, I could always check that out with the NASD.

Shortly after our meeting, I did, and was told he passed his supervisor's test (Series 24) on July 12, 1985. If true, then Koskinen was not licensed to conduct the duties as department head for nearly a year. No big surprise!

After some small talk, I baited him. I mentioned that I had been kicked out of NSI for refusing to be dragged into securities violations. I filled him in on what had happened during the 1975 Mitsui bond underwriting, suspecting that might loosen his tongue.

It did, but not in the way I expected. Koskinen dug into his understanding of pop psychology and began expounding on his theory of personalities. He said, "There are two types of people—Type A and Type B. Type A believes there are differences between people, and this causes misunderstandings leading Type A people to think the other person is either crazy or evil. Since you know the other person isn't crazy, then he is evil. In the Type B personality—and I am Type B—a person believes that deep down everybody is the same and you must work hard to come to an understanding, even if you must weaken your position."

I guessed he was trying to tell me that if I had capitulated on the Mitsui underwriting, things would have turned out differently. What insight, but he may have been right.

When Koskinen was finished, he sat back and smiled at me.

I told him, "Listen, I'm Type A. But personalities have very little to do with my experiences. You either obey the law, or you don't. There's no middle ground."

I leaned forward and added, "Both you and I know what's going on at Nomura. Let's not kid each other. They don't deal above the counter. I was ordered to violate the law. I refused."

Koskinen finally opened up a little. He admitted that he too had been instructed to do things that weren't legal more than once when he first arrived at NSI, but he had refused to go along with anything improper. "When I explained it to them," he said, "they understood and didn't ask me again."

The one thing I couldn't figure out was why Koskinen left NSI. He had been rumored to be pulling down upward of $1 million a year. People don't normally walk away from that kind of pay.

When I felt him out, Koskinen told me that after the October

1987 stock market crash, Tokyo clamped down on his operations and imposed all sorts of trading restrictions. As a result,
he said, he felt he could no longer do the job he had been hired
for, and he tendered his resignation, effective February 1989.
Koskinen said NSI's senior management was quite surprised
by his decision, and he quoted Kurokawa as telling him, "We
thought you were one of us."

Some of the things Koskinen revealed seemed to support
what I heard from another ex-NSI *gaijin* named James Michael
Flanagan. Flanagan had been hired by NSI in May 1986 to
service the institutional accounts he had covered out of the
London office of the Security Pacific Bank. He lasted until
October 1987, when he was dismissed for "failure to meet
draw." Wall Street salespeople are paid either a salary plus
bonus or strictly commissions. If he's on commission, the salesperson usually receives a monthly advance against future earnings. This is called a "draw," and if the salesperson
doesn't generate enough commissions in buying and selling
securities to cover this draw, eventually he or she will be let go.
In a nutshell, that's what happened to Flanagan. But there was
a bit more to his story than that.

Flanagan claimed that when the people in Nomura's London
office discovered he was covering "their clients" from New
York, they let out a howl and invoked territorial rights.
Flanagan was stripped of his British-based accounts, and his
revenues plunged.

Flanagan faced another slight problem. He told me that NSI
used his securities salesperson's license as a cover for some of
its unlicensed salesmen. Flanagan learned of the ruse because
NSI gave out daily commission reports to its salesmen, and
Flanagan didn't recognize a number of credits on his commission runs. Since these trades were for American corporate
bonds, not U.S. government securities, Flanagan's area, he
became suspicious and questioned the items.

He said that his superiors, Robin Koskinen and Koichi Kane,
told him, "You are the only one here with a Series 7, and those
trades belong to an unregistered salesman. If the NASD comes
in here, Nomura would be in trouble, so we're using your
number. At the end of the month, those commissions will be
journaled out and you'll get paid for what you produce."

I checked out the salesman he mentioned. The person passed the NASD Series 7 exam to sell securities on November 18, 1986, and passed the general securities examination for New York State on May 1, 1989, almost three years later. Flanagan claimed the person's commissions appeared under his credit for May, June, and July of 1986.

Once he was dismissed, Flanagan sued NSI for wrongful termination and had his day in court at a New York Stock Exchange arbitration hearing in April 1989. He lost. But Flanagan told me that Koskinen revealed at the hearing that NSI had used Flanagan's license to conceal securities transactions of unlicensed NSI salesmen.

Besides speaking with Koskinen and Flanagan, I had lunch with a former back-office vice president of NSI. He had left a good job with the New York Stock Exchange in May 1986 to join the company. He lasted, however, only until May 1988. He was yet another *gaijin* who felt his dismissal wasn't justified. He claimed he had been made the scapegoat for NSI's second "net capital violation" in two years. The SEC requires member firms to maintain a maximum ratio of indebtedness to liquid capital of 15 to 1. A violation occurs whenever the debt becomes higher. The purpose of the rule is to protect customers and creditors from financial losses should a broker topple.

The ex–vice president told me that NSI's first encounter with a net capital violation was discovered during the NYSE's 1987 review of NSI's 1986 year, the period, curiously enough, in which Nomura successfully captured a primary dealer appointment from the New York Federal Reserve Bank.

The man said that orders came tumbling in from Tokyo to build up NSI's U.S. government securities operations so the firm could gain the primary dealer status. He said volume soared overnight. One of the rules, however, is that a broker must close its books by the end of the working day. NSI didn't have the personnel or the facilities to comply, so yesterday's business was swept into the following day's work. It only compounded the problems as days rolled into weeks and weeks into months—and then along came the NYSE examiners.

He said that when the exchange discovered NSI's bookkeeping problems, other infractions also surfaced. Because of the mess in its back office, NSI was not able to keep track of its capital, and its debt ratio soared past the legal limit of 15 to 1. NSI fell into a net capital violation, which is a serious matter. To top things off, the vice president said, the firm had failed to register the new department with the exchange.

(In the summer of 1990, Nomura paid for these infractions. The New York Stock Exchange censured NSI and fined it $180,000, one of the stiffest penalties ever leveled against a Big Board member firm, for violating net capital requirements and failing to register the division of the firm involved in U.S. Treasury securities, among other infractions.)

Naturally, I was keenly interested in how NSI managed to build up its securities trading operations to qualify as a primary dealer. So I asked the man, "Where did NSI get its business? Was it from Tokyo, from clients, or from internal trading?"

"A lot came from Tokyo," he said, "a little from clients— Nomura really didn't have any clients—and the rest from trading its own account."

I put the same question to NSI's former syndicate associate, Dick Gibson. "It was mostly from one pocket to another," was his succinct reply.

I asked Gibson if he knew the meaning of "wash sales." A wash sale is the purchase and sale of the same security either simultaneously or within a short period of time to give the appearance of activity.

"Yes," Gibson said.

"Then was NSI doing wash sales?"

"Yes."

I spoke to another ex–NSI vice president about the firm's government securities operations. He said, "There is no way that Nomura's volume could qualify it as a primary dealer. I walked down there several times to watch their operations, and I tell you, they didn't qualify." The man had held several high-ranking positions with such firms as Paine Webber and First Boston, so he must have known what he was talking about.

According to my luncheon companion, the NYSE monitored the firm's activities and forced NSI to cut back its operations until it got its house in order.

All of this notwithstanding, after Koskinen hired his first trader in January 1985, business picked up because Japan began buying U.S. Treasury bonds in great quantity. By the fall of that year, NSI made its move. It filed an application with the New York Federal Reserve Bank to become a primary dealer of government securities.

A boulder, however, was thrown into NSI's path, or so it would seem. Congressman Charles E. Schumer of New York had been displeased for some time with the refusal of the Japanese to allow American securities firms equal opportunities in Japan. So when he heard of NSI's latest move, he and thirty-six fellow members of the House Banking Committee signed a petition calling for the rejection of the applications of both Daiwa Securities and NSI, until American-based securities firms were given equivalent treatment in the Tokyo capital markets. The letter was dated October 30, 1985, and addressed to the president of the New York Federal Reserve Bank, E. Gerald Corrigan.

Time ticked by while NSI was apparently getting its act together to qualify as a primary dealer. The Americans were still frozen out of Tokyo, and there was no visible movement to make any changes in the status quo. Despite all these negatives, however, the Federal Reserve appointed both Daiwa and Nomura as primary dealers on December 11, 1986—just in the nick of time for Japan to buy nearly one-third of the upcoming U.S. Treasury's auction.

Corrigan, in comments made to the press, explained that he threw the doors open to the dealers because the United States needed to show the way in opening markets. It was the same shopworn cliché Wall Street had been hearing for years.

To his credit, Schumer kept after the Japanese. When the Omnibus Trade Bill of 1988 was passed by Congress, he attached a rider giving the Japanese until August 1989 to open up their markets, or else they would lose their primary dealerships. Once more, Corrigan rallied to their defense. This time he was joined by Federal Reserve Chairman Alan Greenspan. Both issued strong letters of support for the Japanese dealers.

This support may seem a little peculiar, but there was one possibly pertinent fact that the newspapers never picked up. Corrigan, Yoshitoki Chino, the chairman of Daiwa Securities, and Setsuya Tabuchi, the chairman of Nomura, are all members of the Trilateral Commission, which describes itself as "a private North American–European–Japanese initiative on matters of common concern." Corrigan, it would seem, was just taking a little initiative on a matter of common concern.

While Nomura was buttressing its beachhead in the United States, however, its repeated securities violations and mistreatment of its *gaijin* professionals were finally triggering a backlash. Some people were getting ready to spill the beans.

17

Blowing the Whistle

Ten years earlier, in January 1979, Lou Riggio read an article critical of Morgan Stanley in *Institutional Investor* magazine that impressed him quite a bit more than most articles he saw in the business press. It was perceptive and well researched, with a bite to the style. He decided he would contact the writer and try to pique his interest in another, much juicier story, one he figured would be irresistible to any financial reporter—the story of Nomura's inventive ways of doing business.

At that point, Riggio was not Nomura's foremost fan. Like me, he was amazed by the company's relaxed attitude toward rules and regulations. The shabby way he had been treated by most of his superiors hadn't done much for his morale or sense of loyalty, either. He had been walking a tightrope for years, not really knowing from one week to the next whether he was going to miss a step and go tumbling. The easy thing, naturally, would have been just to leave and work for someone whose integrity you could admire. Unfortunately, it wasn't easy finding other employment during those times. Riggio did in fact begin looking on the sly in 1975, during a period when Wall Street was in retrenchment. He very nearly landed a job with Goldman, Sachs. The firm was decidedly a bit player in South America, and Riggio's contacts there would enable it to become a sizable factor in fairly short order. However, after putting Riggio through many seemingly hopeful interviews, Goldman, Sachs apparently decided it didn't care how much business it did in South America. That was a big disappointment, but Riggio shrugged it off and continued his search. While he had his lines out, he made another decision, which was that it was about time to leak the Nomura story.

The *Institutional Investor* reporter was immediately interested in what Riggio knew. After spelling out the details, Riggio referred the reporter to me. I was nervous and wasn't really ready to go public with my own experiences, but I told Riggio I would be glad to offer some background to a trustworthy reporter. As it turned out, I became his primary source. To his credit, though, he managed to dig up quite a few other Deep Throats on his own.

Alas, despite his own considerable enthusiasm, the reporter ran into what seemed like an insurmountable hurdle in his organization. First of all, there was an editorial debate about the appropriate place to run his story. Besides *Institutional Investor* magazine, the parent company also publishes several weekly newsletters, one of which is the *Wall Street Letter*. Although the reporter worked for the magazine, the vote was to give his story to the newsletter. At that point, a classic Catch-22 developed. The editor of the *Wall Street Letter* advised the reporter that he would publish his story only if the SEC were investigating NSI. To him, that was the story. Scarcely able to believe what he was hearing, the reporter argued that the crux of the story was NSI's violation of securities laws; what difference did it make whether or not the company was being investigated for its misdeeds? The judgment of the editor, however, prevailed. I'm no editor, but I found the logic pretty perplexing. I can hardly imagine a city editor, upon being told that a reporter had the goods on a mass murderer, responding, "No way we run a story until we find out the cops have made an arrest."

Undaunted, the reporter gathered up his package of documentation and paid a visit to the New York office of the SEC. The man he saw was Michael Gregg, the associate regional administrator for enforcement. In pretty short order, the reporter got the distinct impression that Gregg wanted nothing to do with either him or NSI's alleged violations, though he couldn't figure out why. You would think nothing would get the juices of an enforcement official flowing better than some hot tips or wrongdoing. In the end, Gregg made no commitment, but he did express an interest in chatting with some of the reporter's sources. In early August of 1979 I got a call from him.

When I spoke to Gregg to set up a rendezvous point, I asked him, "What do you look like?"

Gregg said, "I am the best-looking guy at the SEC!"

That didn't give me a great deal to go on, but I was still able to pick him out of the crowd. Looming slightly over six feet tall, he had sandy, bushy hair and wore horn-rimmed glasses—not my idea of a matinee idol.

We went to Hoboken for drinks and a little talk, settling on a place near the old Erie Railroad station called Schaefer's. Gregg had a few laid-back questions for me, but he took no notes. I thought this was somewhat odd. Maybe he had a tape recorder in his tie? After a while, however, it became apparent that Gregg was there more to satisfy his own curiosity than to start an investigation.

Over our drinks, I confirmed much of what the *Institutional Investor* reporter had passed on to the SEC. I covered NSI's failure and refusal to license personnel, its market rigging, and its underwriting violations. Gregg showed absolutely no interest. It was as if he had heard it all before. Of course, he had.

Toward the end of the meeting, I had a question of my own. Back in November 1977, Al Barbara had told me that the SEC was investigating NSI's sales of the Japanese foreign bills. Barbara was always very well connected and picked up all the good rumors on Wall Street, so I gave credence to anything he said. I said to Gregg, "I've been hearing all sorts of rumors that you were investigating Nomura's sales of foreign bills of exchange."

"That's right," Gregg answered right away.

That perplexed me. "You had them cold," I said. "Why didn't you do anything?"

The answer really shook me. "The State Department asked us to cease and desist," he said. "So we did."

I couldn't help wondering what this country was coming to.

A year after I met Gregg, in 1980, I decided to try to get to the bottom of the mystery. I wrote the SEC requesting the file on the investigation under the Freedom of Information Act.

In response, Ed Zaval of the SEC called my home and left a message. He said the SEC didn't understand my request. I found this strange, very strange. I had sent a simple three-paragraph letter. Why should that prompt a personal telephone call when a brief return letter would have done?

I returned the call and was referred to an Edward Wilson. I repeated what was already in the letter. A few days later, I received a written reply. The SEC said there was no record of such an investigation. Why would Gregg lie and say there had been one? My mind drifted to thoughts of Watergate.

The years droned by, eaten up by the rigors of my new job, but my interest in Nomura remained as strong as ever. I wanted to talk to Gregg again, so I called and invited him to lunch. It was a brisk October day in 1986 when we settled in at the Mai Tai, a Chinese place in the financial district. When I broached what was on my mind, he confirmed that the State Department had asked the SEC to halt its investigation of Nomura's sales of the unregistered U.S. Treasury instruments.

"Were you involved in this investigation?" I asked.

"It was somebody else," he said, "but it was general knowledge in the office."

I told him about my letter and about the strange telephone call. Gregg straightened up in his chair and leaned forward; he was acutely interested. Now he had a few questions of his own. He wanted to know some more details. Then he settled back in his chair and we finished lunch.

I did have one more question for Gregg: "How come the SEC said there was no file?"

"That could be," he replied with a shrug. "The SEC may not have asked the right person or looked in the right place. Besides, there are no longer any records. After three years, all the files are destroyed."

I suppose that explained it. Meanwhile, the *Institutional Investor* reporter never did get his story in print. Despite what the reporter had shown the SEC and what I had told them, the agency chose not to act. As far as the newsletter editor was concerned, that meant there was simply nothing to write about.

Riggio and I both felt discouraged by the chilly reception our disclosures received, but figured perhaps we were just going about things in the wrong way. In any event, Riggio had a job to worry about and a job hunt to continue with.

As for me, things had gone smoothly enough at Sanyo—I was doing splendidly, and my bosses were pleased with my performance—until trouble walked through the door in December 1984. It materialized in the form of Takayuki Sumitomo, a hard-boiled, twenty-two-year veteran of Nomura Securities. Taka, as he liked to be called, was probably the most Westernized of all the company's Japanese in the United States, having graduated from a California high school and from the University of Southern California. In 1984 he had been transferred from the Los Angeles office to New York. Nine months later, he was "transferred" once again, but this time to Sanyo as executive vice president.

Almost from the day Sumitomo joined Sanyo, he needled me mercilessly, mostly over petty items. But one day in April 1985 he threatened me. Taka stood in the middle of Sanyo's office, turned slightly sideways, put his left fist on his slim hip, shook his right index finger in my face, and said, "I know all about you at Nomura and I know what you did to them. We'll get even with you!"

Within a matter of months, the threat became reality. In June 1985, Taka was made chairman of Sanyo Securities America. In October, with no warning at all, I was passed over for a pay increase at the company's annual employee review. Taka's explanation was: "You have no initiative."

To bolster his statement, he referred to something that had happened three weeks before. Sanyo had been notified that one of its underwritings was the subject of a class action suit. It's not uncommon to be the target of such suits when you've underwritten a stock offering and the stock goes down. It's just one of many occupational hazards. When a suit is filed, the normal procedure is to turn over the notice to the legal department or an outside law firm. Apparently having no idea what the proper routine was, Taka asked me, "What do you do with this notice?"

I told him to send it downstairs to our lawyers.

Taka didn't think too much of that advice. He decided it would be wiser to simply conceal it, so he ordered me to file the notice.

During our meeting, Taka said, "See! The correct way to handle a class action suit is to file it. Your suggestion to turn it over to our lawyers shows you have no initiative." He shook his head and added, "I'm very disappointed in you."

If Taka wanted to be foolhardy and conceal lawsuits, that was his prerogative. But it certainly didn't show any lack of initiative on my part. He said there were other instances, but when I pressed him for examples, he retorted, "We don't have to tell you. You are senior vice president, you should know."

Taka wasn't quite finished. He added, with a touch of sarcasm, "You'll never see another pay raise."

If that was some new technique to motivate employees, it didn't work with me. Figuring my career wasn't looking too bright, I then inquired about Sanyo's pension plan, which had been approved for the local staff in late 1981. As it turned out, it had never been implemented. "You have profit sharing," Taka said with obvious delight. "That is it." My share, for eight years of employment, amounted to a piddling $4,500.

I asked Taka, "Am I to understand that I must rely on myself for my future because Sanyo will not?"

The chairman leaned over and spat out a single word: "*Yes!*"

I tilted my head, looked at Sumitomo, and pointed my finger at him. "You've just made a big mistake," I said.

I felt that, since the long arm of Nomura Securities had reached into my Sanyo career, it was no longer in my best interest to sit on the NSI story. It was time to start spreading the word far and wide.

18

The Keystone Kops

THE JULY 26, 1986, ISSUE OF *BARRON'S* PUT THIS TITLE over one of its letters to the editor: "The Keystone Kops." The letter was written by Lou Riggio, and it painted a black picture of how Nomura Securities behaved in order to further its own interests. By now, as you might remember, Riggio was gone from Nomura. In early 1982, he quit to take that position in São Paulo, Brazil, with the U.S. Commerce Department. After some two and a half years there, Riggio moved to southern Florida, where he started his own company, Accuracy Associates International, a consulting firm in international trade and finance.

In his letter Riggio listed four items that should have been of keen interest to any securities law enforcer: "Their problems [Nomura's senior management's] of a chronic nature include (1) a lackadaisical (to be polite about it) approach to proper registration of sales and supervisory personnel (Good luck on your exams, fellows!); (b) immigration irregularities; (c) management's disdain for compliance matters; and (d) a 'sorry no' record in equal-opportunity employment."

For all the stir it caused, the letter might as well have been written on the winds and printed in invisible ink. Absolutely nobody seemed to take any notice. I decided to help things along.

In November 1986 I sent a photocopy of the Keystone Kops letter to Congressman Charles Schumer. In a cover note, I pointed out that since Riggio was a well-respected, twelve-year veteran of NSI there might be some meat to his troublesome allegations. Schumer was my first choice to alert because, in his role as a member of the House Banking Committee, he had been championing equal treatment for American brokers in Tokyo and had vigorously opposed Nomura's application to become a primary dealer.

I received no acknowledgment.

Because I feared my correspondence had gotten buried in the heavy holiday mail, I called his office and spoke to a young man who identified himself as Al Kaufman. Sure enough, he confirmed that he hadn't seen the letter and asked that another copy be sent.

I mailed it off, and I still heard nothing. In January I called Schumer's Washington office again to talk to Kaufman. This time I was passed along to another aide, Tom Friedman, who said he was the person handling matters having to do with Japanese primary dealers. He said he had never seen the letter and asked that yet another copy be sent.

It was getting a little ridiculous, but this time I finally got an acknowledgment, signed by Congressman Schumer himself. He politely thanked me for my interest and concluded on a "don't call us, we'll call you" note. Wonderful.

I wondered if Schumer was more consumed with snatching newspaper headlines than actually trying to construct a level playing field for American brokers in Japan, not to mention in the United States. With that rude brush-off, I figured the congressman wasn't interested.

Fortunately, I had hedged my bet. I had also sent a letter to a member of the Senate Banking Committee. The man I picked was then-Senator Lawton Chiles of Florida (now governor), and again for what I thought was a good reason. Riggio was now one of the senator's constituents, and while Riggio had been in Brazil he had met him.

Because of this relationship, my letter was taken with somewhat greater seriousness than that offered by Congressman Schumer. However, it still took a phone call to nudge the senator's staff into action. They finally approached Riggio, and he referred them to me for greater details on Nomura's practices.

One day I got a call from John Hilley of the senator's office. We had a brief, cordial conversation, and I was told someone would be contacting me shortly. In March 1987 I heard from John Hilley again and from his two assistants, Mark Logan and Susan Latham. Once again, I confirmed Riggio's allegations and ran through the highlights of a number of NSI's wrongdoings. I also told them how to go about verifying the charges.

Over the next few months, I kept in touch with Hilley, but I heard nothing more from the other two. I was later to learn that Hilley's chief function on the senator's staff was tackling the inordinate complexities of the federal budget, not investigating misconduct by some Japanese brokerage house. Senator Chiles was also chairman of the Senate Budget Committee, so Hilley's intermittent interest was understandable. The weeks turned into months. In time, the senator announced his retirement from Congress due to stress, and his plans to relax on the shuffleboard courts got in the way of any further investigation of NSI.

By now I was getting a little discouraged. Didn't anyone want to know about NSI's crooked personality? Didn't anyone want to put a stop to it? In December my spirits picked up a bit when I received a phone call from a friend who said he knew some people in Washington who would like to hear my story. He asked me to send him some material chronicling the misdeeds at NSI. By now I had lost confidence in the SEC and Congress, but I said, "Sure, if it can be of some help." I still had my doubts. This time, however, I was wrong.

A call the following February advised me that Congressman John Dingell's Oversight and Investigation Subcommittee wanted to meet with me in Washington.

Meanwhile, I had arranged to see another person who harbored an interest in NSI, the former regional administrator of the SEC's New York office, Ira Lee Sorkin.

Sorkin was now a lawyer with the firm of Squadron, Ellenoff, Plesent & Lehrer. He looked like an Ivy League fullback, standing over six feet and weighing at least two hundred pounds. He boasted gray unruly hair that flopped over his forehead like bangs and an ingratiating smile. As he squeezed himself into his desk chair, he asked, "So what do you want to tell me about Nomura Securities?"

Our talk lasted an hour and twenty minutes, and in the end

he told me more than I told him. He said he didn't know of the SEC's supposed investigation of NSI in 1977; that was before his time. However, he did divulge some details of a 1984 SEC investigation involving NSI that was on his watch. At that time, NSI was one of six brokers that had been victimized by a company specializing in investments and taxes. It seems the company had bought and sold nearly $20 million of securities without bothering to pay for the shares. In Wall Street lingo, this is known as free-riding. The case was said to be the largest free-riding scam ever to come to the attention of the SEC (plenty of lesser ones never got that far).

Free-riding, naturally, is very much against the law. This doesn't mean plenty of people don't give it a shot. To pull off the scam, a crooked investor needs a cooperative party within a brokerage house. After finding this partner in crime, the customer proceeds to buy a stock and give Broker A a check to pay for it. The inside person at Broker A will record a payment in the customer's account, but not deposit the check. Next, the investor sells the stock through Broker B, hopefully for a profit. Because Broker A appears to have been paid for the securities, it will deliver the shares to Broker B. The client will take Broker B's check from the sales of the securities and deposit it to cover the check drawn to Broker A. So long as the stock market goes up, such a game can go undetected indefinitely—and generate some eye-popping profits. Unfortunately, as we all know, stocks have an annoying habit of also going down, and most of these schemes collapse when the customer's losses become too big to cover.

This is what happened to NSI. Its client, the investment company, began buying and selling securities in April 1983 through NSI and five other brokers. In February 1984, when losses started to pile up in huge numbers, the fraud unraveled. The client had racked up a $400,000 loss. NSI's share was nearly $160,000, more than any of the other brokers lost. The SEC probe determined that the client had been working in collusion with one of NSI's *gaijin* credit managers, and the SEC censured the firm for lack of supervision and lack of compliance. It didn't surprise me to hear there was a rotten egg in NSI.

Sorkin had more to reveal. "Nomura had no compliance—no compliance manual, no system, no procedures, no checks, no cross-checks, no follow-up," he said. "And each department operated on its own."

I was amazed. "What do you mean, Nomura had no compliance system?" I said. "I hired Andy Basile in 1976 as compliance officer."

"It didn't," Sorkin said.

"Then what happened?" I asked.

"We recommended a law firm to Nomura to come in and set up compliance procedures," Sorkin said.

The thought crossed my mind: By 1986, Nomura Securities International had been an NASD member for seventeen years and an NYSE member for five. It had four U.S. offices, employed 430 people, carried 15,225 customers' accounts, had 92 salesmen, and operated from a capital base of $128 million, making it the twenty-ninth largest American broker. And it had no compliance system!

Over the years, I had seen a lot. But even to me, that was shocking. Then another thought struck me. All the SEC did was recommend NSI hire a law firm to institute compliance procedures. Given what had happened and the circumstances surrounding Nomura's position, all sorts of alarms should have been going off. Instead, the SEC played deaf and mute. I thought, what kind of investigation was this? If a third-grade New York City detective had any hope of making second-grade detective, he would have had probable cause to probe deeper into Nomura. Its operations had gone unsupervised for almost twenty years.

March 3, 1988, was one of those bright, crystal-clear, cool days that make you glad to be alive. But it wasn't only because of the beautiful weather that I was feeling cheery and hopeful. The time had come for my appointment in Washington.

My meeting was with investigators Peter Stockton and Bruce Chafin of Congressman Dingell's subcommittee, which, as one of its responsibilities, oversees the SEC. I entered the Sam Rayburn Building a few minutes early and proceeded to Room 2323. The two investigators took me down a flight of stairs, past Rep. Dingell's office, to a room across the hall. It was one of those hearing rooms you often see on television. There were several rows of chairs to the right, and to the left was a dais for congressmen. Between the two were several long conference tables. The room was deserted except for a cleaning woman. She quickly gathered up her gear and disappeared through a doorway on the far side of the room. Stockton and Chafin took the side of the table near the chairs, and I arranged myself with my back to the dais. Clearing his throat, Stockton opened the meeting by saying, "So what do you want to tell us about Nomura?"

Before I answered, I had a request. "I want an understanding that I am to be protected," I said. "I want complete confidentiality and anonymity."

"You've got it," Stockton shot back.

That was a load off my mind. I didn't have to look over my shoulder for security leaks.

I had carried some papers with me from New York and organized the contents into a folder the night before. Out came Lou Riggio's Keystone Kops letter from *Barron's*. That was the lead-off batter.

I went over Nomura's violations as laid out in the letter, as well as some other instances of underwriting misconduct. At one point, Stockton didn't seem satisfied with what I had to say and, probably to draw more out of me, snapped, "You're withholding information."

I leaned forward and replied, "No, I'm not. There's a lot to cover. I've brought all my information with me. See, I've got it in this folder. Here it is." I flicked the folder across the table to him. "I brought it for you—keep it."

Next, I related the story of Nomura's illegal sales of the unregistered foreign bills. Stockton seemed totally uninterested. When I was done, he shrugged his shoulders and asked, "Who's been hurt?"

I couldn't believe it. Here I was, sitting in a congressional hearing room on Capitol Hill, a place where the laws of the country are forged, reporting violations of those laws, and an investigator was asking me, who's been hurt?

I turned to Bruce Chafin and asked, "What's the mortgage rate on your house?"

He looked young, and I figured he probably paid top dollar. I was surprised by his answer.

"Nine percent," he said.

"Oh, you got it years ago," I said.

He nodded.

I swiveled around and asked Peter the same question. He gazed off to his left toward the empty visitors' chairs, shrugged, chuckled, and replied, "Higher."

"You can thank Nomura for that one," I said. "They ran up your mortgage rates."

Stockton stopped smiling. I had just told him who had been hurt. Him. And he suddenly got serious. I went on and mentioned my encounter with the SEC and the alleged cease and desist request from the State Department.

Chafin asked, "Why would the State Department ask the SEC to cease and desist from an investigation?"

My answer got a rise even out of him. It was as if somebody else had taken over. I said, "There may have been a $1 million check given to the Democratic party."

"Whaaat?" Stockton said.

I had a reason to think so. In March 1980 I had lunch with Sue Robbins in the basement restaurant at 55 Water Street. Robbins and I had become acquainted because our daughters were friends and classmates at P.S. 6 in New York, a great school at an unbeatable price. Later, Robbins and I worked together for the same brokerage firm before going our separate ways. I went to the Japanese and Robbins went to Bear Stearns.

Robbins was working in retail sales, selling stocks and bonds to individuals. However, she had something extra going for her. A friend of hers was a big-time fund-raiser, and they used to take each other to one another's functions. Robbins took her friend to Wall Street receptions so she could mingle with the moneyed people of finance who could and would make hefty contributions to worthy causes. The friend would in turn take Robbins to various fund-raising events so she could meet wealthy individuals with deep pockets for investing.

During our luncheon, Robbins told me of her friend's frustrations. A law had recently been passed restricting individual contributions to politicians to $1,000. That meant she had to scratch much harder to raise money; how well she did affected her own pocketbook, because she worked on commission.

Foreigners, however, were not covered by the new law, so they suddenly became far more attractive game. And if you bagged one, Robbins said, you wouldn't believe the sums to be had. To illustrate this, Robbins told me that her friend's company had recently received a check from a Japanese company for $1 million. It was presented in the company's Madison Avenue office to the owner of the fund-raising firm. "The Japanese made a ceremony out of it," Robbins said. "The check was wrapped in gold paper with a bright red ribbon tied around it, and all the Japanese were bowing."

"When did this happen?" I wondered.

Robbins squinted as if solving a problem and said that it had been about a year or two ago. That would have put it just about the time the State Department allegedly interfered with the SEC.

Later on, I thought I had put two and two together, so I phoned my old SEC friend, Mike Gregg. I opened the conversation by saying, "Mike, are you still the best-looking guy at the SEC?"

"Naturally," was his answer.

"I found out why the State Department asked your agency to cease and desist from your investigation of NSI. It's bigger than any of us thought, and you were right to lay off. A friend told me there was a $1 million check passed by the Japanese to a political party."

Mike feigned a Southern accent and said, "Thank you, Mister Jimmy, thank you." Carter, you recall, was president at the time.

Not long afterward, I met Sue Robbins's fund-raiser friend during *Institutional Investor* magazine's three-day conference at the New York Hilton Hotel. I attended the afternoon session of the second day, where investment opportunities in Japan were to be discussed. I had absolutely no interest in the presentation, and the president of Sanyo had even less. But he dragged me to the meeting because he was keen to meet potential investors, and this seemed the place to find them. Our session broke up at about five o'clock, and we headed for the door. It was one of those strange fateful moments. I spotted a bulletin board out of the corner of my eye. There was one lonely notice stuck on it, an invitation to attend an open house at the Goldman, Sachs penthouse suite.

I tugged on my president's arm and said, "Look. If Edward

Goldstein [the Goldman, Sachs vice president covering the Japanese brokerage accounts] found out we were here and didn't attend his party, he would be very disappointed."

That was all I needed to say. We swung away from the exit and strode toward the elevators.

The party was just starting to warm up when we arrived. Quickly, we fell into the festive mood. A couple of hours later, I spied Sue Robbins. Even though she didn't drink, she was in the company of several pretty hard-drinking female friends. One stood out from the rest. She was a tall, willowy, blowsy redhead with the flash and sparkle of the Gabor sisters. Her trademark was a long cigarette holder. She was none other than Robbins's high-powered fund-raiser.

The women and I gravitated upstairs to the penthouse, found a cluster of chairs and a sofa, and settled in. The fund-raiser naturally held court. I'll give her this, the woman knew how to captivate an audience, and she regaled us with unfailingly amusing stories.

Somehow she learned that I worked for a Japanese company. By this time, I had possibly had one drink too many but I recall her griping about the difficulties of raising money for political candidates. She went on to tell a story about a group of Japanese men who presented her company with a check for $1 million, just like the guy in the old TV series "The Millionaire."

Just about that time, I looked up and saw my president coming our way, his eyes lit up. He was quite fond of ladies. I missed the conclusion to the story, and the conversation swung to other topics.

I was totally wiped out the next day and didn't make it to work. It was a Friday, so I had the weekend to recover. I waited until the beginning of the next week to confirm what I had heard at the Goldman, Sachs reception. I called Robbins, who said of her friend, "She has a big mouth when she's been drinking."

I asked, "Did she say what Japanese company gave that check?" Robbins replied, "Nomura."

Later, I tried several times to confirm the donor's identity with the fund-raiser herself, but to no avail. She proved oddly evasive. Although she never did confirm it, she never denied it, either.

Without the cigarette holder or the potent drink, I did my best to relate the story to Stockton and Chafin. But since I didn't want to lead them astray, I cautioned them, "There is probably no way to run this one down, so don't try. The fund-raiser claims she doesn't remember anything, and if there were any files, she says they don't exist today."

We returned to the alleged 1977 SEC investigation of NSI. Again, I stressed that there would be no way to completely corroborate it, because if it had happened, the official files were by now destroyed. "So don't try to prove these stories," I said. "Believe me, there are a lot of other things to go after."

Stockton and Chafin stood up. Stockton stuck out his hand and gave a firm handshake. "The SEC is going to have a lot to answer for," he said.

I never spoke to either of them again.

19

More Keystone Kops

OVER THE SUBSEQUENT WEEKS, I HEARD NOTHING DI-rectly from the Oversight and Investigation Subcommittee, but I did get some sense of where matters stood. The aides had been impressed enough with my revelations to take the story to the general counsel of the subcommittee. He, in turn, pre-sented it to John Dingell, who felt the allegations sounded grave enough to order a probe of NSI.

It's one thing to order an inquiry. It's quite another to find someone to carry it out. Dingell could locate no available sub-committee investigators, so a body had to be requisitioned from the General Accounting Office. My understanding was that the investigator was going to work full-time on the Nomura case.

With the deliberate way the federal government works, it took two and a half months to get the investigation going, but things really started percolating in May. At that time, I was contacted by the GAO investigator, a stolid man named Bill Hill. I also learned, much to my delight, that another GAO man, Rich Chervenak, had been added to the probe. We set up a meeting for one o'clock on the afternoon of May 18 at my suburban New York house.

At one on the dot, my doorbell rang. Standing there were two studious-looking men flashing credentials. Bill was slim and nondescript, his manner as lusterless as his dress. Rich was older, much larger, and resembled an older version of the late actor Richard Boone.

When the appointment was arranged, I had been advised to

197

have whatever evidence I possessed on hand and be prepared to name people who could back up my charges. I had done my homework. Over the prior few days, I had wracked my brain and come up with more than sixty names. I figured that should keep the investigators busy, and I assumed they would pick up more on their own.

The three of us arranged ourselves in the dining room. They extracted small pocket notebooks, plopped them on the table, and stared expressionlessly at me. I stared back. This routine was entirely new to me, and I didn't know the protocol. I had been forewarned that they knew nothing about Wall Street or securities regulations, which gave me a sinking feeling.

To get things going, I pulled out Riggio's letter and attempted to explain the technical aspects of the alleged wrongdoings. I did the best I could to broadly frame the scope of NSI's violations and then handed over my lengthy list of names. "You'll basically find two types of people here," I said, "ones who have stories of wrongdoings and others who know about abuse of personnel. And that in itself could lead to additional information."

We methodically covered my list name by name. Neither man had a single question. Was I getting through to them? My concept of an investigator was someone who grilled you so long and hard that you needed a full bottle of Extra-Strength Tylenol once they finished. Not these guys. They passively listened and said nothing.

As the clock approached three, Bill announced that they had to get going because he had a plane to catch to Charleston, West Virginia; he commuted from there to Washington. In leaving, they said they would keep in touch, and we shook hands. I never heard another word from them either.

I did, however, hear indirectly of their halting movements. Lou Riggio telephoned me a few days later to let me know that Bill Hill and Rich Chervenak were headed to Florida to visit him the next day. He called afterward to fill me in on the meeting. He said the investigators spent three hours with him, and he basically backed me up right down the line, confirming all my allegations. But then he mentioned something a little disconcerting. "They told me to call them if anything else came to mind," Riggio said. "I did recall something and called their hotel. They weren't in, so I left a message. They didn't call back."

Once again I had to wonder: Didn't anybody care about NSI? Was the world nuts?

If nothing else, the investigators were accumulating some good frequent-flyer mileage. A week later, Sue Robbins called from Seattle, where she was now working, to tell me she had a lunch date coming up with Hill and Chervenak. I was glad she called, because it gave me the opportunity to remind her about what they were poking into. "They're interested in the $1 million check story," I told her. "I hope your memory is a little better than mine. I had a lot to drink that night."

"Don't worry," Robbins consoled. "My friend talked about it at several parties. That wasn't the first time I'd heard the story."

A few days later, I got two calls from Seattle. The first was from Sue, and the other was from Fred Coleman, the ex–NSI mutual fund portfolio manager. Robbins said she had seen the investigators and everything went smoothly, adding, "I dropped the Dingell boys off at an office building, and after that they were on their way to Los Angeles."

Fred Coleman told me that he too had just seen the investigators. "I did a number on Jack Wallace," he said, still holding a grudge. "I told them that when I started working for NSI in San Francisco, they rushed me out to take the registered principal's test because they didn't have anyone registered," he said. "They told me I was to be the office principal."

That was the first time I had heard that story, though I wasn't surprised. I had done some snooping around the San Francisco office and discovered that Chikayasu Ito, the senior vice president and resident manager of the office, was deficient as a New York Stock Exchange branch manager because he had failed to complete the required training period. He also lacked the required NASD principal's and California state securities licenses.

After those calls, I remained guardedly optimistic that the investigation would progress, until I heard the final chapter from none other than Andy Basile. (Basile's NSI career ended in 1987, and he accepted a position as vice president with

Sanyo Securities America. By 1988 we had known each other for eleven years.) Late in June, six weeks after the probe had been launched, Bill Hill called Basile. I don't know Hill's side of the story, so all I have is what Basile told me. As he recounted it, "The phone rings, and this guy's on the phone yelling at me. He tells me he's from the Energy and Commerce Committee, and they are investigating Nomura Securities. He says, 'Where you been? I've been calling you for days.' Well, I told him, 'What do you mean? I got better things to do than wait for a phone call I didn't know was coming. I'm busy.' So he says, 'I'm downstairs in a phone booth, and we're coming up to see you.'"

Basile stopped them dead: "I told them, 'No way. You're not coming up here.' Then this guy said, 'We'll subpoena you.' I told them to go ahead, there's a long line. The guy slammed down the phone."

Basile said that he hurriedly passed the word to NSI that it was being investigated by John Dingell. In short order, he was summoned to a meeting with top management and the company's lawyers. NSI, according to Basile, accused him of blowing the whistle, but he swore he would never do such a thing and reminded them he had even signed papers pledging his silence. "If I'd talked to them," he told the executives, "I wouldn't have told you about the investigation."

At that point, the Dingell investigation came to a screeching halt. Later on, I learned that the subcommittee was stalled because it felt it was unable to confirm my allegations and couldn't get enough people to talk about NSI. I was dumbfounded. I had told them that the only areas that would be a waste of time to pursue were the $1 million check story and the SEC investigation. Otherwise, I knew of only one person who wouldn't talk. Many of those on my list weren't even called. As far as I could tell, the investigators only pursued the two items I suggested they not bother with.

Another person I phoned, a *gaijin* vice president who had been laid off by Nomura, had this story to tell: "I came home one day and there was a message on my answering machine. It was the Oversight Committee, and a telephone number was left. I called Washington and got the right office, but the person wasn't in, so I left a message. They never returned my call. I signed a contract saying I won't talk about Nomura, but I would love to be subpoenaed. I'd tell everything. They never made an honest dollar—believe me, they haven't."

He went on to relate the events leading up to his own firing: "Toward the end of the year, I was given a stack of orders to approve. I signed a few and noticed something strange. The trades were phony. It was an income tax evasion scheme. Nomura was skimming profits off London and parking them in New York." In 1987 Nomura International London reported earnings of $100 million, while Nomura New York lost nearly $15 million, yet the vice president said London's earnings were actually higher and New York's losses were larger. Nomura had to pay taxes on its profits in London, but not in New York. "I said, no way, I'm not signing this. I reported it to the compliance guy, Peter Chepucavage. He started shaking. He's a real nice guy. He cried when I was fired."

I said, "I heard a rumor that Nomura paid off your contract in full."

"Yes," he replied. "I think I could have gotten more, because when I sat down to negotiate it, they jumped on my offer so fast it made my head swim."

Time passed, and the investigators vanished into thin air. I heard through the grapevine that they needed more help, so I wrote what was to be the first of a string of letters once again detailing NSI's alleged violations. I laid out the allegations and listed the people who could confirm them. I got no response.

I thought: If nothing else, I must be well on my way to setting a Guinness world record for reporting violations.

One thing I found strange was the apparent difficulty they were having in proving that NSI's people were unlicensed. That was a cinch. All they had to do was visit the SEC's New York office and ask for NSI's public records. All brokers must list their officers on a form called Schedule A of Form BD. Armed with that list, any investigator could check it against the information on file at the National Association of Securities Dealers' registration center in Rockville, Maryland.

In fact, I did just that myself. In October 1988 I walked into the SEC public information office on the tenth floor of 26 Federal Plaza in New York City to take a look at the NSI file. I got a surprise. The last full accounting of all officers, from chairman to assistant vice president, was dated September 6, 1985. There were several later filings, the last one dated July 10, 1987, listing only the senior officers. This confused me, so I asked the lady sitting behind the desk if she could explain the difference. She picked up the telephone, dialed a number, asked for Alex Worabeck, and handed me the receiver.

Worabeck identified himself as an SEC examiner. I said, "I have a question concerning the Form BD. Does a broker have to list all officers or just senior officers?"

"All," he said.

"When you say all, do you mean from the chairman down to an assistant vice president?" I said.

"Yes," Worabeck replied. "The job has nothing to do with it. If a firm does not register its personnel, they are in violation of the law. But we can't be like a fly on the wall and watch each move. We must rely upon the brokers to keep their lists updated."

I thanked him, hung up the telephone, and returned to my office. The next morning, I called the SEC just to double-check, and it confirmed Worabeck's story. I started to understand why anybody looking into the NSI operations had difficulty figuring out who its officers were: They weren't listed.

On November 7, 1988, I wrote a letter to Peter Stockton, Bruce Chafin, Bill Hill, and Rich Chervenak summarizing what I had discovered. First I pinpointed people with interesting stories to tell. Then I mentioned a few facts about NSI's existing licensing problems. Working from a copy of the firm's latest internal telephone directory, I could identify only twenty-two of the fifty-four officers listed in the 1985 filing. The directory included more than two hundred officers. What's more, twenty-nine officers registered on the 1985 SEC Form BD—and still considered, in the eyes of the SEC, officers in place—were no longer in the 1988 telephone directory. Among the missing in action were Yoshio Terasawa, identified in the SEC filing as NSI chairman; Akira Shimizu, listed as president; and Yoshio Nitta, executive vice president. I knew they were long gone from New York, but according to the documents filed with the SEC, they were still running the show at NSI.

There were a few notable holes as well. I pointed out that the current president, Katsuya Takanashi, was unlicensed as a principal officer from December 1986 to April 1988. According to the NASD records, Takanashi hadn't filed his application for a license with the NASD until he was seventeen months into his job. It took another five months before he filed his papers for approval with the New York Stock Exchange. Then there was Chikayasu Ito, senior vice president and identified in the SEC filings as resident manager of NSI's San Francisco branch office, who was listed by the NASD as a deficient NYSE branch manager for failing to complete his required training period, and also for having no California state securities license. Makoto Takahashi, senior vice president and chief of fixed income sales and trading, had no supervisory license or state approval on file with NASD. Shinji Ohyama, vice president and chief of the syndicate desk, had no state licenses, and Hiromasa Takaura, another vice president, had no supervisory license.

I got no response to my letter.

I did, however, hear from Lou Riggio. Riggio had a job interview with the federal government in Washington during the last week of Feburary. He arrived just in front of a winter blizzard but was able to keep his appointments; in fact, he wrapped up his business early. This allowed him some free time for an unscheduled trip to Room 2323 in the Rayburn Building, the office of the Oversight Subcommittee.

Riggio said Hill and Chervenak took him down the hall to a private room. Once seated, they told him the sorry news that the NSI probe had been dropped in favor of greater concentration on the insider trading investigations launched in the wake of the Ivan Boesky scandal and, as Riggio put it, "on a really irrelevant software-purchase boondoggle by the National Guard." The investigators apologized, but added that they had no say in the matter; their agenda was set by Representative Dingell.

After I learned this, I sent a letter to Representative Dingell expressing my disappointment and asking for an explanation. None came.

My typewriter was wearing out by now, but a few months later I wrote one final letter to John Dingell. I gave him some

additional information I had assembled on NSI, and I concluded: "Congressman Dingell, each individual act of wrongdoing
by Nomura Securities International can, in itself, be boiled
down to being trivial, to being technical, or to the ultimate cop-
out—'who's been hurt?' However, taken in their entirety of
nearly twenty years of systematically violating our securities
laws, they add up to a totally different dimension. The gravity
is undeniable. If these actions are not worthy of your attention,
then, in my humble opinion, these securities laws are not
worth enforcing."

This time I got action. I received a copy of a letter sent to
David S. Ruder, chairman of the SEC. My letter had been
forwarded to him along with instructions to have someone look
into my allegations and report back. Several months passed,
but I heard nothing further.

There was one notable development unrelated to my correspondence. In August the *Wall Street Journal* carried a story
headlined "Honda Stock Trading Prior to Report Spurs Probe
by British Market Officials." A few days earlier, Honda had
reported that its six-month earnings had tumbled a whopping
40 percent from the prior year. Its stock had been under "unusual activity" before the report became public knowledge, and
the British were trying to determine whether any insider trading had taken place. I checked into the story on this side of the
Atlantic and was told by the director of research at a smaller
Japanese brokerage house that the Honda people in New York
were furious with Nomura. He told me that Honda said,
"Somehow a Nomura securities analyst in London had estimated a 40 percent decline in Honda's earnings to the penny
and had given it out at a meeting of investors." This allegedly
happened two days before the report.

I contacted the Japanese desk of a major American securities
dealer in New York and asked if it could explore the story with
its London office. I got my answer the following day. It confirmed what I had heard from the research director, but the
American firm's London people didn't know anything about
an investors' seminar. I passed this tidbit on to an old friend
with the financial press who had been following NSI for some
time. From time to time, we had swapped information on NSI.
She had, in fact, furnished me with sources and documents

that confirmed some of the infractions I suspected. Then I sat back to see if the story got published. It didn't.

In early September I called to find out what was developing on the Honda lead. The reporter had not been able to pin anything down, but she wanted to talk about something else. "Why have you been feeding all my information to Dingell?" she asked.

I was confused. "What?" I said.

"Why have you been passing the information I've given you to the Dingell committee?" she repeated.

Something was wrong—very wrong. I had never told the reporter that I had been in touch with the Dingell people, and they had promised me anonymity.

I said, "I visited the Oversight and Investigation Subcommittee in March 1988, but the investigation was dropped this past February. I'm not denying it."

"You can't deny it," the reporter said. "I'm looking at your letter."

At first, I thought the letter was the one Dingell had sent to the SEC, but it wasn't. It was mine to Dingell. I asked where the letter was sent from and got a terrible surprise. "By fax from our Washington office," she said. "They got it from Dingell's office."

My cover was blown. My correspondence had been handed out to the press and I'd been burned. It was time to get moving and publish the book about NSI's business activities on Wall Street.

Since the time I had joined it, NSI had grown substantially mightier. By 1990, Nomura Tokyo's official capital base was a stunning $9.8 billion. Japanese accounting standards, however, tend to be very conservative. Most companies' assets are carried on their balance sheets at cost, or purchase price, and don't reflect their true market value. Nomura is no different in this respect. Therefore, it isn't surprising that experts place Nomura's real capital base at around $80 billion. How does that compare to Wall Street? *Business Week* recently estimated that the entire American brokerage industry's capital stands at less than $40 billion. That means Nomura is nearly twice the size of all of Wall Street put together!

The firm has become a daunting money machine. With profits of $2.2 billion, Nomura became Japan's biggest moneymaker in 1987, surpassing traditional leader Toyota, and ranked as the sixth most profitable company in the world. Nomura's income was double that of any of its financial competitors, which all happened to be Japanese—Dai-Ichi Kangyo Bank, Sumitomo Bank, and Daiwa Securities. The best showing any American company could muster was the $583 million earned by American Express, just over a fourth of what Nomura made. With the beating that the Japanese stock market took in the last few years, Nomura's profits have shrunk somewhat, and its pretax profits fell to $1.7 billion in 1990. But everyone expects that before long it will return to its past earnings glory.

Every number you look at tells a similar story of incredible dimensions. The market value of Nomura's shares has risen as high as $66 billion in recent years, as much as thirty times the value of Merrill Lynch's.

Breathtaking as these figures are, Nomura's strength and power remain in its roots—the retail Japanese customer. There are more of them than ever. So many, in fact, that Nomura handles roughly 17 percent of all stock trades done in Japan. Along with its full-time sales staff, Nomura continues to employ a force of twenty-six hundred part-time saleswomen who march from door to door peddling stocks and bonds, the descendents of the feisty midis who distributed the savings chests after the Second World War. But to grow in the future, Nomura knows, it must become a more global behemoth, and that means nurturing the thirty-eight foreign offices it has planted in twenty-three countries. Because Nomura manages assets of nearly $400 billion, it has no choice but to turn outside Japan for diversification and deployment of its clients' capital. It must exploit the world's financial markets, and there is little reason to think it won't. Its current president, Yoshihisa Tabuchi, who took the helm in 1985, is intensely ambitious. To safeguard its clients' assets, Nomura must be able to dominate and even control any market it enters. If you own the casino, you make your own rules, and the odds always favor the house.

With Nomura's power and its devil-may-care attitude toward rules, it seems only a matter of time before it will fulfill most of its worldwide ambitions. After six years of operation, for instance, its London subsidiary has already moved to the front in the Eurobond market, displacing such long-standing titans as Deutsche Bank and Credit Suisse First Boston. If its record in New York is any indication, one can assume there's more to that growth in Europe than meets the eye as well.

Whether Nomura will ever solve the muddling ways of its American affiliate is problematic. Though NSI has become a mighty force in the U.S. Treasury bond market here, it continues to report losses or only tiny profits. Not that it doesn't keep trying new things. NSI shocked Wall Street in the summer of 1988 when it announced it was laying out $100 million for a one-fifth stake in the flashy, red-hot merger and acquisitions firm run by the rumpled Bruce Wasserstein and his less visible partner, Joseph Perella. That move paves the way for Nomura to pick up precious knowledge in corporate raiding, and undoubtedly will enable it to assist its Japanese clients in snapping up American companies, an area in which NSI has been traditionally weak.

More significant, in October of 1989 Nomura did the improbable by hiring a *gaijin* to head up all of NSI. The man the Japanese recruited was Max Chapman, Jr., a sturdily built, intense man who had been president of Kidder, Peabody & Company. Eager to fit right in, he quickly began reading books such as *Japanese Made Easy* and *Learn Japanese in Two Weeks*.

But it wasn't very long before Chapman began to sense what he was up against. It was bad enough when he found out his cramped new office overlooking the East River on Maiden Lane had until recently been a visitor's waiting room. So he didn't think it altogether unreasonable to request a matching sofa and chairs to replace the wretched rented furniture. But after a month with the same ugly stuff in his office, he inquired about progress. Chapman was told clearance had not yet been given for his order. Several more weeks went by. Each time Chapman asked, he got noncommittal answers. Finally, he summoned the man assigned the task and shoved his business card in his face. "See the card?" Chapman huffed. "I'm the chairman, all right? I can order some furniture."

He had a lot to learn about the Japanese. He got another fast lesson when he took a trip to visit his Tokyo bosses. While he was meeting with them one day, to show he was very much in the Nomura spirit, he casually asked for one of the Nomura lapel pins all Japanese employees so proudly wear. Sorry, he was told, that was entirely out of the question. The rules are quite clear. Only employees of the Tokyo parent company can get a lapel pin.

Epilogue

O<small>N</small> O<small>CTOBER</small> 25, 1990, <small>MY DAYS AS AN</small> A<small>MERICAN IN A</small> Japanese brokerage house ended for good. Day after day, Takayuki Sumitomo, Sanyo Securities America's chairman, had continued to nitpick everything I did. Ever since his ominous threat to "get even" with me, I had felt I was living on borrowed time—and I was right. One by one, my duties were reassigned to young, inexperienced Japanese nationals who had little knowledge of the English language and less of the American securities markets. All I was left with was our underwriting activity. The pay raises I got were less than half the company average, and my year-end bonus was cut—even as I moved Sanyo into first place in underwritings among the Japanese firms.

None of this mattered. Sumitomo's threat was no idle one. On October 25 I was handed a written termination notice.

Since November of 1990 I've been a program director with a tax-exempt foundation in New York. My latest assignment is a project to bring Soviet executives to the United States for three- to six-month internships with American companies.

Since my old friend Lou Riggio left NSI in 1982, he has passed through several incarnations. As I have mentioned, from 1982 to 1984, he was U.S. consul for commercial affairs in São Paulo, Brazil, managing an office of trade specialists and coordinating programs with Brazilian authorities. As his appointment was ending, he organized the Ex-Im Bank's Program Pro-Brasil. Since 1984 Riggio has headed Accuracy Associates International, a Florida firm promoting trade with Brazil. He also is the U.S. representative for Platense, Ltd., of São Paulo, a leading Brazilian sporting goods company, and functions as an advisor in international finance and trade to the Caribbean Development Bank and as a contract interpreter for the Department of State.

We need to wake up to the reality that we are in an economic war with the Japanese. To protect the integrity of our securities markets, we should take a close look at the Japanese brokers who have invaded our shores. And, if we are going to permit the Japanese to conduct business here, we must also get them to unlock the doors to their markets and let us compete over there as well, be it in securities, automobiles, electronics, or computers. After all, Japan offers the second largest market in the world, and the most profitable for those companies who service it.

If the United States government is truly dedicated to creating equitable opportunities in global finance—and I'm not sure it is—it should take steps to close the doors to foreign interlopers that slam their doors on us. Maybe that is the only way to get them to believe in an open market. The importance of an open, competitive global market can't be underscored enough. There are only three major financial markets in the world. As of early 1991, 80 percent of the worldwide value of securities rested in America, Japan, and the United Kingdom. About 37 percent was here, 32 percent in Japan, and 11 percent in the United Kingdom. By keeping foreigners at bay in Tokyo, Japan enables Nomura to keep billions of dollars of profits for itself, while protecting it from foreign competition. Money is power, and as Nomura builds its already huge capital base from this privileged perch, it gains the financial wherewithal to crush whomever and whatever gets in its way.

It's bad enough that we allow the Japanese into our markets without first assuring equal treatment for our companies in Japan. But what's worse is that we don't then require them to live in our country by the same rules and regulations that govern American firms. It's as if we actually want to give away the store.

How much longer will our government ignore violations of our securities laws by Nomura? Are our leaders now too terrified to stop Nomura for fear that without it, billions of dollars of U.S. Treasury bond issues would go unsold? Or is it that we are so naive as to think that because the Japanese have not yet made truly profitable inroads on Wall Street, they never will?

Once again, it seems, the Japanese are picking our pockets while we go whistling on our way. We've already lost the electronics industry. Automobiles are no longer the exclusive province of Detroit's Big Three. Will our financial community be the next to fall to Japan?

Maybe this book will open some eyes before it's too late. I hope so.

Index